PT BOAT SQUADRONS
US Navy Torpedo Boats

SPEARHEAD

PT BOAT SQUADRONS
US Navy Torpedo Boats

Angus Konstam

Ian Allan
PUBLISHING

Acknowledgements

Design: Compendium Design
Maps: Mark Franklin

Note: Internet site information provided in the Reference section was correct when provided by the author. The publisher can accept no responsibility for any subsequent changes to the sites.

Above: *PT-32* formed part of the squadron stationed in the Philippines immediately before the Japanese invasion of the islands. The boat was destroyed on Tagauayan to prevent her capture while escorting General MacArthur to safety. (US Navy)

Right: PT boats speed through Pollog Harbor during the landings on Mindanao, 17 April 1945. (National Archives)

First published 2005

ISBN 0 7110 3044 8

Published by Ian Allan Publishing Ltd

an imprint of Ian Allan Publishing Ltd, Hersham, Surrey KT12 4RG
Printed in England by Ian Allan Printing Ltd, Hersham, Surrey KT12 4RG

Code: 0502/A2

British Library Cataloguing in Publication Data
A CIP catalogue record for this book is available from the British Library

CONTENTS

ORIGINS & HISTORY

Above: The classic PT boat: *PT-552* was an 80ft Elco boat which was originally built for delivery to the Russian Navy, but which was transferred to US Naval service while she was being completed in May 1943. She was finally delivered to the Soviet Navy in April 1945, after serving for 18 months under the American flag in the Mediterranean and the English Channel. (PT Boat Museum)

Although the first self-propelled torpedo was pioneered just after the American Civil War, the US Navy (USN) had only just begun to develop its own fleet of motor torpedo boats (MTBs) when the Japanese attacked Pearl Harbor. Due to a combination of naval doctrine, budget limitations and sheer dogma, the USN almost missed the boat. Fortunately the experimental work undertaken while Europe was already engulfed in a world war paved the way for the creation of America's own fleet of patrol torpedo boats (PTs), which entered service just in the nick of time. These superb little craft would go on to play a significant part in ensuring Allied victory in the war at sea, but the path that led to the creation of this 'mosquito boat' fleet was a rocky one.

When the British inventor Robert Whitehead pioneered the use of the torpedo as an offensive weapon in 1866, he revolutionised naval warfare. Unlike mines or 'moored torpedoes', his 'locomotive torpedo' could be used against specially selected targets, such as enemy battleships and large cruisers. His first weapon was powered by compressed air, had a speed of 6 knots and a range of less than 500 yards. However, by the time he offered his design to the world's naval powers three years later, his design was much more powerful, and boasted a device which kept it on a relatively steady course and depth. The British were the first to adopt the torpedo, and in 1876 they produced HMS *Lightning*, the world's first torpedo boat. Other nations followed Britain's lead, and as both torpedoes and torpedo boats improved, naval tactics developed to cope with the new device. By the 1880s the weapon had gained a loyal following among naval theorists, particularly the adherents of *la jeune école* (the young school), who adopted the doctrines espoused by the French Admiral Hyacinthe Aube. He argued that the torpedo meant that the days of the battleship were over, as one of these prestigious and expensive warships could be sunk by a relatively inexpensive torpedo boat, thereby obviating the need for the battleship. Torpedo boats could dominate coastal waters, rendering a country immune from amphibious attack or enemy bombardment. This view was the antithesis of that held by Capt Alfred Mahan, an American naval historian and theorist who advocated the pursuit of 'seapower'. Mahan saw the battleship as the arbiter of naval victory, and this view was shared by both the USN and the Royal Navy — after all, they had the battleships. The experiences of the British and Americans in World War I only served to underline their belief in the Mahanian doctrine of seapower, as it was by the use of the British battlefleet that the Germans were eventually brought to bay, their coastline blockaded and their population starved into surrender. The only element of *la jeune école* doctrine to make a mark was the use of submarine warfare to threaten the sea lanes of the large maritime powers. After the war, while both the British and the Americans were willing to develop their own small submarine fleet, they appeared to ignore the possibilities of developing their own fleet of small torpedo boats. After all, they had both experimented with these craft before, and had found the vessels wanting in strategic purpose.

In 1887 the USN's first torpedo boat, USS *Stiletto*, entered service, followed by several more vessels or classes in the decades which followed. During this period naval designers invented the 'torpedo boat destroyer' as an antidote to the torpedo boat; small warships which could screen the main battle fleet from attack by torpedo boats, and sink the attackers through gunfire. Inevitably the distinction between torpedo boat and torpedo boat destroyer became blurred, and by World War I most destroyers were also fitted with torpedoes. This development was coupled with a general increase in the size of destroyers, and an increase in their armament from light quick-firing guns to weapons with a calibre of 75mm (3in) or more. While many naval powers experimented with small torpedo boats during World War I, in almost all cases these fleets were disbanded when the war ended. This created a gap in the naval arsenal for light, fast motor boats armed with torpedoes.

During the interwar years, US naval strategists regarded motor torpedo boats as unsuitable vessels for inclusion in their Mahanian fleet. With the exception of the fledgling aircraft carrier arm, they were building a fleet based on the experiences gained during World War I, where the firepower of battleships and long-range cruisers would be the arbiter of naval victory. For them, MTBs had no place in a 'blue water' navy. However, during the late 1930s naval analysts became alarmed by reports of developments in Germany and Italy, where both countries were building up powerful motor torpedo boat forces, based on the designs of interwar speedboats. It was, therefore, decided that the USN needed its own motor torpedo boat design, if for no other reason that its existence could provide a counter for this new threat.

By the 1930s the USN had already developed its own fast motor launch designs, but these had not proved suitable for adapting into motor torpedo boats. Consequently the USN needed a new type of fast motor boat, specifically designed to carry torpedoes. The concept of the MTB found an ally in President Franklin D. Roosevelt, who helped persuade Congress that these boats were vital to American naval interests. Indeed, when a budget was first allocated, it was left at the discretion of the President how it should be spent! He wisely left the decision to the USN.

In 1938 Congress added an extra $15 million to the USN's annual budget, specifically for the development of these prototype torpedo boats, which they defined as vessels

Alfred Thayer Mahan (1840–1914) and **Hyacinthe Laurent Theophilus Aude** (1826–1890)

Mahan graduated second in his class from the Naval Academy in 1859 and went on to serve in the Federal Navy during the Civil War — spending most of his time on blockade duty. He joined the Naval War College, Newport, RI, in 1884, becoming chief instructor and president.

Mahan made two main contributions to naval theory. The first was based on his studies of the Royal Navy and the contribution of British sea power to its victory over Napoleon. He went further: he said that sea power was an essential requirement for any nation that wanted to be a great power.

The second was his emphasis on the battleship and the concentration of naval forces into a main battle fleet. To Mahan, the destruction of the enemy's fleet was the main objective — a theory that influenced naval building before World War I and the strategies of the war. It also had a huge impact on British and American naval doctrine during World War II, a fact that could have been exploited by the Nazis had they concentrated on submarine warfare rather than trying to rebuild their battle fleet.

On the other hand, Hyacinthe Aude spent many more years at sea, distinguishing himself through personal bravery and ability. He came to writing late, but in 1882 published *La guerre maritime et les ports militaires de la France*, which propounded the theories of *la jeune école*, based around speed, small vessels and the demise of the battleship. Minister for the Navy from 1886, his building programme proved to be weak on design — but the value of his theories became obvious during World War II.

Above: The birthplace of the PT boat: Bayonne, New Jersey, the site of the Elco shipbuilding plant where 398 PT boats were built during the war . (Elco)

displacing less than 3,000 tons. This gave the USN the latitude to develop larger, ocean-going torpedo boats if they wanted, more akin to the torpedo boats developed in the days before the advent of the destroyer. However, after some discussion the USN opted for a smaller type of vessel, similar to the craft being designed in Europe, and capable of being produced quickly, and in large numbers if required. Although these would be incapable of crossing the Atlantic and Pacific Oceans under their own power, it was expected that these craft would be transported to any future theatre of operations, and then let loose upon the enemy. The USN launched a competition, and sent out specifications for two sizes of MTB, a 54–60ft and a 70–80ft boat. While both were armed with two torpedoes, the armament of the larger boats was more substantial, with 20mm guns as well as machine guns mounted on deck. Both sizes of vessel were expected to have a top speed of 40 knots, and a range of 550 miles. Even more significantly, both vessels were meant to have as small a displacement as possible, — ideally less than 20 tons — allowing the vessels to be winched aboard most cargo ships and carried as deck cargo.

It was a tall order, but 37 private firms rose to the challenge and submitted designs. During the interwar years several boatbuilding firms had developed fast speedboats of the type the USN now wanted, although a major impetus for this interest was prohibition. Organised crime groups used 'rum runners' to bring illegal alcohol into the country through the Great Lakes from Canada, across the Florida Straits from Cuba, and up the Atlantic seaboard from the Bahamas. The USN was simply finding a legitimate need for these designs of fast speedboat. In addition, the demand for luxury fast speedboats was growing on both sides of the Atlantic, and playboys and millionaire yachting enthusiasts commissioned their own designs. This meant that many American firms were well aware of speedboat developments in Europe and amongst their competitors, and could be relied upon to furnish the boats the USN now realised it needed.

In late 1938 a shortlist was drawn up of eight designs from the 37 proposals submitted to the USN, and following the submission of more detailed plans, two designs were selected, one for each size of boat. In March 1939 the contract for the 54ft patrol torpedo (PT) boat was awarded to the design team led by the gifted naval designer Professor George W. Crouch, who had established a fine reputation as the designer of record-holding speedboats such as *Typhoon* and *Cinderella*. The 70ft contract went to the renowned New York boatbuilding firm of Sparkman & Stephens. Both winners were awarded a prize of $15,000, a significant sum at a time when America was struggling to emerge from the depression. Within two months the USN had signed contracts with three boatyards to build six prototypes based on the two designs. These six boats would become *PT-1–PT-6*, and with their inception in May 1939, the US Naval PT boat fleet was born.

READY FOR WAR

Of the first six PT boats the USN commissioned, four would be based on the smaller George W. Crouch design, while the last two followed the plans developed by Sparkman & Stephens. *PT-1* and *PT-2* were both 58ft long vessels, built by the Fogal Boat Yard of Miami, Florida. Although both hulls were launched in late summer 1939, neither boat was completed before late November 1941, by which time the designs were considered obsolete. This was due to delays in the production and installation of their Vimalert V12 'Liberty' petrol engines. The vessels were almost immediately reclassified as small boats, and served as naval tenders. *PT-3* and *PT-4* were more successful, and both 58ft vessels were completed by the Fisher Boatworks of Detroit, Michigan in June 1940. However, although they were both powered by powerful Packard engines which gave them a top speed of 32 knots, the USN found them to be too small. Another design flaw was that the torpedoes fired backwards, over the stern, which limited the effectiveness of the vessels. After evaluation, both craft were transferred to the Royal Navy in April 1941, becoming MTBs 273 and 274. They spent the war in Canadian waters. While Professor

Below: PT boats often adopted "V" formations while attacking, as this guaranteed a degree of visual contact between the boats during an approach, and the formation could react quickly to unexpected developments. (PT Boat Museum)

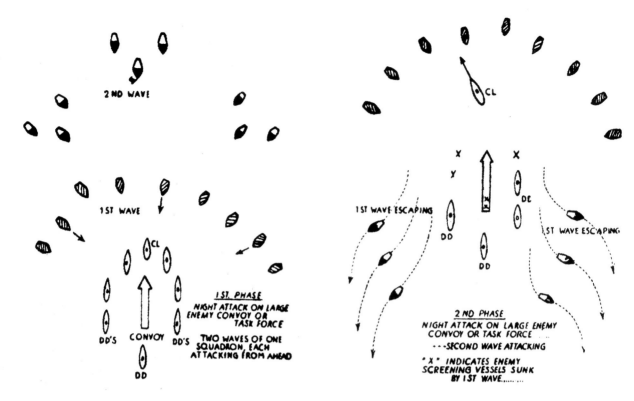

Above: PT boat commanders were trained to fight their boats both individually and in groups. Here the USN guide to PT boat tactics outlines the method of engaging a convoy using two whole squadrons of boats; attacking in two waves, then escaping into the night to allow the second wave to approach their targets. (National Archives)

Crouch could build great speedboats, it seemed that his designs were less suited to the needs of the USN.

The last two boats of the May 1939 commission were both built along the lines of the plans submitted by Sparkman & Stephens. *PT-5* and *PT-6* were both 81ft boats (a foot longer than the original specifications), and were built by the Higgins Industries Boatyard of New Orleans, Louisiana. Unlike the 58ft boats which displaced 20 to 25 tons, these boats had a displacement of 34 tons apiece, making them distinctly heavier than the original USN specifications. However, with their distinctive rounded superstructure, unobstructed torpedo tubes and long, relatively spacious afterdeck, their design followed the lines of the later wartime boats. As these were experimental craft, both vessels were fitted with different engines, *PT-5* carrying a Vimalert petrol engine, and *PT-6* a Packard diesel engine similar to those fitted into *PT-1* and *PT-2*. Both vessels were completed in the first months of 1941. More accurately, two *PT-6* vessels were built by Higgins, the first being replaced by the second during construction. The first vessel was first earmarked for the Finnish Navy, and was then transferred to the Royal Navy in June 1940 as *MGB-69*. The final version of *PT-6* was completed in February 1941, a month before *PT-5*. Compared to the lighter, smaller Couch designs, these two boats seemed almost exactly what the USN wanted. They were fast, responsive, and capable of carrying two 21-inch torpedoes. After evaluation was completed in April 1941, the two boats were transferred to the Royal Navy, becoming MTBs *269* and *270*. While the designs for these boats were being studied, the USN finished its own plans for an 81ft PT boat. It was therefore decided to build two more experimental 81ft craft, which became *PT-7* and *PT-8*, following the designs drawn up by the USN's own Bureau of Ships. The hull of *PT-7* was laid down in late March 1939, a month before the contracts were issued for the construction of *PT-1* to *PT-6*. Launched in late October 1940, these two boats were completed in record time, and entered service in late February the following year. As they were experimental craft, *PT-7* was built from wood, while *PT-8* was built using

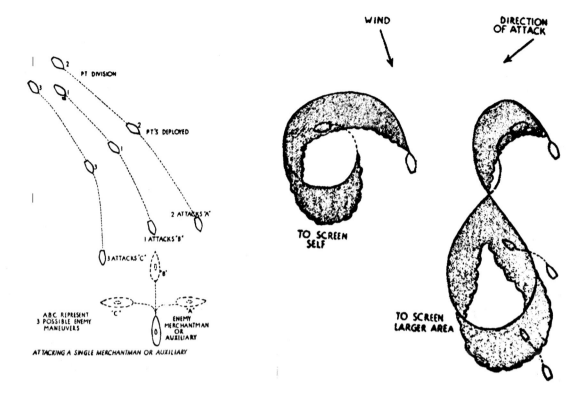

aluminium. Neither were particularly successful, largely because they proved too small to carry anything like the weapons load the USN required. Worse, they also used the stern launch system, which was considered tactically unsound, as the boats would have to approach their target, then turn away before firing, making aiming extremely difficult when under fire. Like most of the other experimental craft, both vessels were handed over to the Royal Navy in April 1941, being redesignated MTBs *271* and *272*. Being considered unsuitable for combat, they were handed over to the Canadian Navy, and were used as air-sea rescue launches. Meanwhile the USN had to go back to the drawing board, as it was left without any suitable design.

The problem with *PT-1–PT-8* was that, due to developments in Britain, they were all virtually obsolete almost as soon as they were completed. A year before the outbreak of World War II in September 1939 the Royal Navy embarked on a crash programme of MTB construction. It called upon the services of several designers and boatbuilding yards, the most famous of which was the Vosper Yard of Portsmouth. Equally important were the designs produced by the British Powerboat Company, many of which had come from the drawing board of its gifted head, Hubert Scott-Paine. Unfortunately Scott-Paine had made enemies in the government, and consequently the majority of contracts for British boats went to Vosper. Unperturbed, Scott-Paine sailed to New York, taking one of his designs along with him. The Scott-Paine MTB was a 70ft wooden-hulled boat with a hard-chine hull, powered by three Rolls-Royce Merlin engines, the same engines used in the Spitfire and later in the Mustang. This gave the 30-ton boat an impressive top speed of over 40 knots. Scott-Paine's boat arrived in New York on 5 September 1939, a week before Britain went to war. President Roosevelt had become a supporter of Scott-Paine, and he had already talked the USN into trying out the British design. In June 1939 the USN struck a deal with the Electric Boat Company (Elco) of Bayonne, New Jersey, who purchased the Scott-Paine boat on behalf of the USN, for experimental purposes. In December Elco also bought the rights to build its own version of the British vessel,

Above Left: When firing torpedoes it was important to engage the enemy at the optimal angle of deflection. This method of attack meant that whatever a target might do, one of the three boats would be in the perfect firing position. See photograph on page 9. (National Archives)

Above Right: PT boats were fitted with smoke protectors, allowing them to lay a smoke screen to aid their withdrawal after launching an attack. This diagram outlines two ways of laying down a smoke screen by both individual boats and groups of vessels. (National Archives)

guaranteeing the production of 23 70ft boats if the USN wanted them, thereby creating two squadrons of 12 boats apiece, including *PT-9*. After the first trials of the vessel in the waters off New York Harbor, the somewhat sceptical team of USN inspectors decided that this was exactly what the USN needed. They had found their PT boat.

The Scott-Paine boat (later designated *PT-9*) was armed with four 18-inch torpedoes, mounted in forward-firing tubes spaced down the length of her hull. In addition she carried two twin .50cal machine guns, mounted in Dewandre turrets sited behind the bridge. Elco retained the boat while they completed plans for the construction of their own Elco versions of the vessel, and *PT-9* was only handed over to the USN in mid-June 1940. This meant that by the summer of 1940 the USN had its first PT boat squadron, consisting of *PT-3*, *PT-4* and *PT-9*. The Higgins boat (*PT-6*) joined the experimental squadron in August, although by that time it was found that there was no comparison between *PT-9* and the other boats, although *PT-6* showed some potential. After all, by this stage the American government was convinced that the country might well be dragged into the war, and Congress had duly approved funds for the production of a whole class of new PT boats. The only workable design the USN had at the time was the Scott-Paine inspired Elco craft, and therefore the New Jersey company was given the contract to start producing these boats in quantity. Elco had embarked on the construction of its first batch of 70ft boats based on the *PT-9* design as early as February 1940, just two months after it signed a contract with Scott-Paine. These boats would eventually become *PT-10* to *PT-19*. Another 12 boats were built to the same specifications, but the USN designated these as PTCs (Motor Boat Submarine Chasers), and then transferred them to the Royal Navy in April 1941, where they became MGBs (Motor Gunboats) 82 to 93.

The first Elco version of the Scott-Paine boat differed slightly from the original British design. First, the Rolls-Royce engines were replaced by three Packard 1,200hp diesels, which would eventually become the propulsion system for all PT boats. The design of the superstructure was made more streamlined, and more stowage space was created. The

Below: *PT-8* and her sister *PT-7* were 81ft boats of aluminium construction, built on an experimental basis at the Philadelphia Navy Yard during 1940–41. *PT-8* was retained by the navy as YP-110, and survived the war to be sold into private hands, and is still in existence today. (US Naval Historical Center)

bridge was lined with aluminium, and the crew quarters were improved. The first of these boats was launched in late August, and the entire batch of 11 boats entered service in November and December 1940. The USN had its first operational PT boat squadron, which it designated MTB Squadron 2, as the 1st Squadron consisted of the experimental boats. *PT-9* was duly transferred, bringing the squadron strength up to its full complement of 12 boats. In February 1941 Squadron 2 (more commonly abbreviated to 'Ron' 2 — so MTB Ron 2) was sent south from New York to Key West, Florida, where the formation was put through its paces. While the performance was satisfactory, several defects were noted, which Elco promised to put right as soon as a new batch of boats was ordered. The USN was about to do exactly that. These first Elco boats were designed to carry British-designed 18-inch torpedoes, but the USN wanted its boats to carry the larger and more powerful home-grown 21-inch Mk VIII torpedo. As the torpedoes were 4ft longer, and the boats were expected to carry two pairs of torpedoes, one on each side of the vessel, the USN decided it wanted longer boats. The Bureau of Ordnance recommended that all new PT boats should have 80ft hulls, but in the interim, Elco had incorporated its own modifications to the original Scott-Paine design, and had come up with a 77ft PT boat. To save time, the USN contracted Elco to produce two more squadrons of these new vessels, 24 boats in total. These boats would be designated *PT-20* to *PT-44*, and would form the basis for the first operational PT boat squadrons of the war. These were the boats which would rescue General MacArthur from the Philippines, and which helped stem the tide of the Japanese advance in 1942.

Meanwhile, Elco was about to discover that it had a rival. *PT-5* and *PT-6* were both built by Higgins Industries Incorporated of New Orleans, Louisiana. This encouraged the company to develop its own PT 'dream boat', a 76ft MTB design which the USN saw, and considered worthy of incorporation into its experimental squadron for further evaluation. It was designated *PT-70*. Another company, the Huckins Yacht Company of

Above: The 70ft prototype motor torpedo boat designed by Scott-Payne of the British Powerboat Company was purchased for evaluation by Elco, and then by the USN, who designated her *PT-9*. In July 1940 she entered service as part of MTB Ron 1, but was transferred to the Royal Canadian Navy in April 1941. This British craft was the direct ancestor of the wartime Elco boats which followed her. (PT Boat Museum)

Above: The interior of the main workshop at the Elco shipbuilding plant in Bayonne, NJ. The latticework nature of the hull construction can be clearly seen, a device which gave the boats great strength and made them less susceptible to heavy damage than more conventionally built vessels. (Elco)

Jacksonville, Florida came up with its own 72ft boat. Both of these experimental craft entered service at the end of June 1941 as *PT-69* and *PT-70*, and over the next two months the USN conducted a series of speed trials off the Rhode Island coast which became known as the 'Plywood Races'. The Higgins and Huckins boats competed against *PT-6*, *PT-8* and five of the new Elco 77ft boats. While Elco emerged as the clear winner, the Higgins boat demonstrated the soundness of its design. Therefore, while Elco was given a fresh order for more 77ft boats, Higgins Industries won a USN contract for the production of 24 of its own boats, which entered service during 1942 as *PT-71* to *PT-94*. These were improved 78ft versions of the original *PT-70* design.

Therefore, by the time the Japanese attacked the American fleet at Pearl Harbor on 7 December 1941, the USN had its first PT boats in service. Within weeks it would order a crash programme of boatbuilding, commissioning Elco to produce an improved version of the 'PT-20' class which would become the 80ft PT boat, the mainstay of the American 'mosquito boat' fleet during the war. Higgins would also be contracted to produce even more 78ft boats, and the company would become the second largest producer of PT boats of the war. As a stopgap in the aftermath of Pearl Harbor the USN also ordered the production of a series of 18 Huckins boats, an improved 78ft version of the mediocre *PT-69* design. Within weeks of America's entry into the war, three American boatyards from New Jersey to Louisiana were in the business of mass-producing the PT boats which would help turn the tide of the war in the Pacific, and which would play a major part in the Allied campaigns in Europe. Meanwhile, the first boats to enter service were already coming under fire.

IN ACTION

Although for various reasons they have become associated mainly with the war in the Pacific, PT boats served in every theatre of operations during the war. They first saw action following the attack on Pearl Harbor on 7 December 1941 and the Japanese assault on the Philippines which took place immediately afterwards. Thrust into the limelight, the PT boats performed with élan in the Philippines, while their evacuation of General MacArthur earned them the admiration of the American public. Although it would be six months before they returned to the fray, PT boats had already demonstrated they could 'punch above their weight' in the Pacific. While this theatre saw by far the greatest concentration of these craft, America's commitment to the defeat of Germany made it inevitable that USN PT boats would make an appearance in the European theatre. Sure enough, Higgins and Elco boats fought alongside the Royal Navy in the Western and Central Mediterranean, and took part in the campaign which saw the defeat of the Germans in North Africa and Sicily, and then the invasion of Italy. By 1944 a few boats had entered service in the English Channel, where they served under the leadership of the man who had saved MacArthur at Manila. By the time of the D-Day landings these boats had been joined by others, and once again, the USN worked closely with the coastal forces of the Royal Navy to clear the seas of German shipping. From Italy to the Philippines, and from Alaska to New Guinea, PT boat squadrons participated in the fight, serving as gunboats, scout ships, escorts, landing craft and supply vessels as well as torpedo boats. These versatile but ultimately expendable craft served as the workhorses of the fleet in every theatre of war, and in the process they made a contribution to the final victory which was out of all proportion to their size and firepower.

Below: A group of 77ft Elco boats in formation, photographed off Hawaii in mid-December 1941. *PT-26* to *PT-30* and *PT-42* formed the basis of MTB Squadron 1, whose first mission was the defence of Pearl Harbor in the aftermath of the Japanese attack on 7 December 1941. (Smithsonian)

Above: The 70ft Elco boat *PT-11* after running aground off the Isle of Pines, an island on the southern coast of Cuba, in spring 1941. She was refloated after all of her stores and weaponry had been removed, and she returned to service in time for her transfer to the Royal Navy in April. (Smithsonian)

Right: Two types of USN. 77ft Elco boats *PT-28* and *PT-29* of MTB Squadron 1 under way off Pearl Harbor in late 1941, dwarfed by the aircraft carrier USS *Hornet*. After Pearl Harbor both boats saw action in defence of Midway Island. (National Archives)

Left: The 70ft Elco boat *PT-12* leading the six other boats of MTB Squadron 2 during a peacetime transit of the Atlantic seaboard conducted in January 1941, as they headed south to Key West, Florida. Three months later several of these boats including *PT-12* were transferred to the Royal Navy. (Smithsonian)

Below: MTB Squadron 2 preparing to sail from New York Naval Base prior to a transit to Key West, Florida in January 1941. These 70ft Elco boats carried twin 0.50-inch heavy MGs in two Dewandre gun turrets abaft the bridge, and four fixed 21-inch torpedo tubes. (US Navy)

Above: The Philippines in 1942 as US forces were
squeezed southwards. The Japanese forces landed in
the north between 10 and 24 December. The US forces
escaped from Manila Bay to Mindanao.

Opposite Above: Lt Bulkeley's *PT-34* in action against
a Japanese transport vessel in Manila Bay during the
night of 18-19 January 1942, in a painting by James
Sessions. The actions of Bulkeley and his men set the
standard by which all subsequent PT boat crews were
measured. (US Navy)

Opposite Middle: Lt John D. Bulkeley USN (1911–96)
commanded MTB Squadron 3 during the Japanese
invasion of the Philippines, 1941–42. He went on to
participate in the naval defence of the
D-Day landings, and retired from the USN in 1974,
with the rank of vice-admiral. (US Navy)

Opposite Below: *PT-34* photographed on the deck of
the USN oiler *Guadalupe* during the transport of MTB
Squadron 3 to the Philippines in late 1941. She
formed part of Lt Bulkeley's squadron which helped
defend Manila Bay, before she was beached and
destroyed in April 1942. (US Navy)

THE PHILIPPINES, 1942

The US Asiatic Fleet based at Manila in the Philippines included
MTB Squadron 3 commanded by Lt John D. Bulkeley. His force
consisted of six PT boats; *PT-31* to *PT-35*, and *PT-41*, with a total
crew of 83 officers and men. This small force would soon face the
full might of the Japanese war machine. The first air raids came on
8 December, the Japanese concentrating on the American airfields
in the Philippines. The landing force appeared the following day,
followed by a concentrated air assault on the naval base. The PT
boats based at Cavite managed to put to sea and avoid the bombs
aimed at them, and gunners even claim to have shot down three
attacking aircraft. Meanwhile the base was all but destroyed, and
the squadron lost its entire stock of fuel and spare parts. After
helping transport the wounded to hospital, the boats withdrew to
a nearby fishing village, where they set up a new temporary base.
It was a difficult time. As the Japanese had full control of the skies,
patrols tended to be undertaken under cover of darkness. The
squadron helping protect Manila Bay itself from any Japanese
landing, and on 17 December the boats helped rescue survivors
from the passenger ship *Corregidor*, which had been trying to
evacuate non-combatants when she struck a mine. *PT-32*, *PT-34*
and *PT-35* pulled almost 300 people to safety that night.
Meanwhile the military situation was deteriorating rapidly, with
Japanese troops advancing on Manila from the north, east and
west. On 22 December General MacArthur declared Manila an
open city, and withdrew his remaining troops to the Bataan
Peninsula. The MTB squadron held its own, performing rudimentary repairs to its boats,
and Bulkeley's men managed to keep all but *PT-32* in action. On Christmas Eve *PT-33*
ran aground and had to be destroyed, reducing the strength of the squadron to just four
boats. The squadron had its first taste of offensive action on the night of 18–19 January,
when *PT-34* attacked and possibly sank a Japanese freighter. Meanwhile *PT-31* had to
be abandoned when she broke down under enemy fire, and three men were lost when
her crew scuttled their boat. With *PT-32* back in action in late-January, the squadron
managed to keep its strength steady at four boats. On the night of 1–2 February she
attacked a Japanese minelayer off the entrance to Manila Bay, damaging but not sinking
her. However, these successes were rare, and as the army continued to give ground on
Bataan, it soon became clear that the end was inevitable. On 23 February the Army
ordered General MacArthur to leave the Philippines and take command of the build-up
of Allied forces in Australia. The squadron would have the job of spiriting their
commander away to safety.

On 11 March MacArthur boarded *PT-41*, accompanied by his wife Jean, their son and
his nurse, and the General's Chief-of-Staff. 13 other passengers were also embarked,
mainly army and navy officers. MacArthur later recalled hearing a conversation on he
dockside; 'I heard someone ask, "What's his chance, Sarge, of getting through?" And the
gruff reply, "Dunno. He's lucky. Maybe one in five".' MacArthur would survive to return to
the Philippines, two and a half years later. As their commander was spirited away the
remainder of the garrison fought on. The last outpost on Bataan would only surrender on
6 April, while the island fortress of Corregidor finally submitted on 6 May. With *PT-41* in
the lead, supported by *PT-32*, *PT-34* and *PT-35* the squadron slipped out of Manila Bay

Medal of Honor Citation
Lt-Cdr John Duncan Bulkeley
Commander MTB Squadron 3

For extraordinary heroism, distinguished service, and conspicuous gallantry above and beyond the call of duty as commander of Motor Torpedo Boat Squadron 3, in Philippine waters during the period 7 December 1941 to 10 April 1942. The remarkable achievement of Lt-Cdr Bulkeley's command in damaging or destroying a notable number of Japanese enemy planes, surface combatant and merchant ships, and in dispersing landing parties and land-based enemy forces during the 4 months and 8 days of operation without benefit of repairs, overhaul, or maintenance facilities for his squadron, is believed to be without precedent in this type of warfare. His dynamic forcefulness and daring in offensive action, his brilliantly planned and skillfully executed attacks, supplemented by a unique resourcefulness and ingenuity, characterise him as an outstanding leader of men and a gallant and intrepid seaman. These qualities coupled with a complete disregard for his own personal safety reflect great credit upon him and the Naval Service.

Above: *PT-41*, the 77-foot Elco boat commanded by Lt John D. Bulkeley, carried General MacArthur and his family to safety in March 1942. The boat was destroyed at Mindanao a month later, to prevent her from falling into Japanese hands. (U.S. Navy)

and headed south in a diamond formation. Progress was slow, as the patched-up engines on *PT-32* and *PT-34* were causing problems. *PT-35* became separated in the dark, and *PT-32* had to put into an island in search for fuel. That left Bulkeley and MacArthur in *PT-41*, and the erratic *PT-34*. On the morning of 13 March the two boats arrived at Cagayan on Mindanao, where the General was airlifted to the safety of Australia, where he would give his 'I shall return' speech. This still left MTB Squadron 3 deep in hostile waters, and far from home. *PT-35* limped in that afternoon, bringing the squadron strength up to three boats. Bulkeley's men made what repairs they could at Cagayan using the limited facilities at the base until he heard news of *PT-32*. The ailing boat was at Tagauayan and was deemed no longer seaworthy. The crew was rescued by a submarine, and the boat destroyed.

Bulkeley's next assignment was to rescue President Quezon, head of state of the Philippines, who had set up his government on Negros. The island was now threatened by Japanese invasion, so leaving the mechanically temperamental *PT-34* behind, he set off from Cagayan to Negros in *PT-41* and *PT-35*. The latter ran aground and had to be left behind, but President Quezon and his family were eventually rescued, then whisked to safety to Mindanao, from where he was flown to Washington D.C. Bulkeley returned to rescue *PT-35*, towing her to Cebu where she was repaired. With *PT-34* back in service Bulkeley now had just two boats left. On the night of 8–9 April he launched an attack against the Japanese light cruiser *Kuma*, each boat firing two torpedoes, which missed their target, or failed to explode. *PT-34* was damaged in the attack, and the following morning the limping PT boat was spotted by Japanese aircraft who bombed and strafed her, leaving her a floating wreck. She was duly beached and destroyed. Three days later, on 10 April, the Japanese captured Cebu, and *PT-35* was destroyed before she could fall into enemy hands. This left Bulkeley in *PT-41*, but on 13 April orders came from MacArthur that he should be airlifted to Australia. Days later *PT-41* was destroyed as the Japanese advanced, and her crew joined the land forces defending the island. The story of MTB Squadron 3 is a heroic one, and one of sacrifice in the face of a superior enemy. Of the 83 men who formed the squadron, 18 were killed and 38 captured, of which a further nine would die in captivity. For his part in the operation, Lt Bulkeley was personally awarded the Medal of Honor by President Roosevelt, the first PT boat hero of the war. More would follow.

THE CENTRAL PACIFIC, 1942

Following the attack on Pearl Harbor the American military became concerned that the next Japanese move would be an attack against the continental United States. Therefore the 2nd Squadron was delayed from being sent into the Pacific in early 1942, but instead was ordered to defend the Panama Canal. While it saw no action, the 1st Squadron did manage to fire a few shots in anger. MTB Ron 1 consisting of 11 77ft Elco boats (*PT-20* to *PT-30*) had been sent to Pearl Harbor a few months before the war began. (Note: The cumbersome squadron designation was usually abbreviated to 'Ron' in all but official reports. In the following account the simpler term will be used, as that was the term used by the crews themselves).

The squadron commander, Lt Clinton McKellar Junior, was well aware that after the demise of Bulkeley's 3rd Squadron, his small force constituted the entire American PT boat fleet in the Pacific at that time. This was a period when the Japanese advance appeared unstoppable. The Philippines, Malaya, Borneo and the Dutch East Indies had all fallen. In Burma the British were being pushed back to the borders of India. The only setback to the Japanese advance came in early May, when an American naval force engaged the Japanese in the world's first carrier battle in the Coral Sea. Although the engagement was a tactical draw with both sides losing a carrier, the loss of the USS *Lexington* was a loss which the Americans could ill afford. Both initiative and numbers still lay with the Japanese.

This all changed in June 1942. The story of the great carrier battle of Midway (4–6 June 1942) lies beyond the scope of this narrative, although McKellar's PT boats played a small part in this great American victory, the turning point of the war in the Pacific. In late May naval intelligence revealed that the Japanese planned to attack the island of Midway, 1,400 miles due west of Hawaii. Reinforcements were sent to help defend the islands, and these included Ron 1. The boats made the long blue water trip under their own steam, arriving shortly before the attack on the island by Japanese carrier aircraft. All the boats survived the attack, despite minor damage to *PT-25*, and the squadron claimed to have shot down three Japanese aircraft. It was the first taste of action for these crews, and the first engagement involving PT boats since the fall of Manila. After the battle the squadron returned to Hawaii, and then a month later it was split into two groups. *PT-22*, *PT-24*, *PT-27* and *PT-28* were transported north to help defend the Aleutian Islands, while the rest of the squadron was shipped to the southwest

Below: *PT-330* was an 80ft Elco boat which served in the Pacific theatre. Her unusual weapons' configuration included a 37mm gun on the forecastle, a 40mm Bofors on the stern, and a 20mm forward of her bridge. (US Naval Institute)

Opposite Above: 78ft Higgins boats off the Aleutians, with the mountains of Attu in the background. Patrols such as these intercepted the supply and reinforcement of Japanese forces lodged in the western Aleutians, then the boats supported the Army's efforts in driving the Japanese from the chain of Alaskan islands. (National Archives)

Opposite Middle: Map of the Aleutians showing airfields and the submarine base at Dutch Harbor. Attu is at extreme left.

Opposite Below: The PT boats operating in the Aleutians proved extremely vulnerable to the appalling weather conditions in this theatre. Here, boats of MTB Ron 16 are shown protected against the sub-zero conditions at their main base on Adak. (US Navy)

Below: PT boats operating off the Aleutians. These 78ft Higgins boats of the 16th Squadron (MTB Ron 16) operated in support of the army's advance along the Aleutians chain from February 1943 until the end of the war. (US Navy)

Pacific. The war had moved on from the central Pacific, and the PT boats moved forward to new bases, where they could take part in the long fight back.

THE ALEUTIANS

The Aleutian Islands in Alaska had been the target of a diversionary attack by the Japanese in June 1942 during the Midway campaign, and the western portion of the chain had been occupied by the Japanese, from Attu in the east through Kiska and to Amchitka in the west, almost halfway along the string of islands towards the Alaskan mainland. Of these, Attu and Kiska had both been fortified and turned into regional Japanese bases. This meant that they relied on supplies brought to the islands from Japan, and the rugged coastline was well suited to torpedo boat tactics in an effort to disrupt this supply line. Consequently Lt McKellar of Ron 1 and his four remaining boats were shipped from Pearl Harbor to Seattle, where they could join forces with the units gathering to reclaim the lost islands. The waters of Alaska were notoriously rough and uncompromisingly cold, but it was felt that the fog banks which were commonly found in the Aleutians would provide McKellar's boats with the cover they needed to launch hit and run raids on the Japanese supply ships. The boats arrived in Seattle on 11 August, and nine days later they set off under their own steam for Dutch Harbor on the Aleutian island of Unalaska. This would be the main base for the coming operation. The four boats completed the 2,500-mile voyage on 1 September, then after a brief rest (where *PT-28* was fitted with radar) they continued on to Adak, where they established a forward PT boat base. The conditions were appalling, as the boats lacked any form of heating save gasoline stoves. Sailors recalled a thick layer of ice formed on the inside of the plywood hulls, while the boats were in constant danger of capsizing through the build-up of ice on their upper decks and superstructures. Two of the four boats were driven ashore in icy squalls, but were hauled off, while *PT-28* was driven ashore and wrecked. These were no conditions for flimsy plywood craft. *PT-22* was shipped home for repairs, but was so badly damaged during the shipping that she had to be scrapped. Therefore, by February 1943, Lt McKellar was left with just two boats to fend off any Japanese invasion attempt. The two boats remained in Alaskan waters throughout the next year, until reinforcements finally arrived and *PT-24* and *PT-27* could be sent home for a much-needed refit. The new Alaskan boats were all 78ft Higgins boats, a force consisting of 12 boats, and designated Ron 13, under the command of Lt James B. Denny. The Higgins boats were better suited to the climate than the 70ft Elco boats they replaced, having both sturdier hulls and proper heating systems. In May 1943 these boats supported the assault on Attu, and after the island was recaptured it became the new forward base for the squadron. For the rest of the Aleutians campaign the boats saw no real action, but acted as rescue boats for downed pilots. The campaign ended three months later when Kiska was assaulted by American troops, who discovered that the Japanese had withdrawn from the islands. By August 1943 the Aleutians were cleared of the

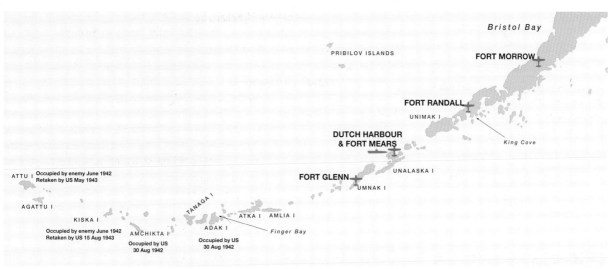

Bristol Bay

FORT MORROW

PRIBILOV ISLANDS

FORT RANDALL

UNIMAK I

King Cove

DUTCH HARBOUR
& FORT MEARS

UNALASKA I

ATTU I
Occupied by enemy June 1942
Retaken by US May 1943

FORT GLENN

UMNAK I

AGATTU I

TANAGA I

ATKA I   AMLIA I

KISKA I
Occupied by enemy June 1942
Retaken by US 15 Aug 1943

ADAK I

AMCHIKTA I
Occupied by US
30 Aug 1942

Finger Bay

Occupied by US
30 Aug 1942

Japanese, and the PT boats stationed in that inhospitable corner of the Pacific could be redeployed where they could continue the fight. Ron 13 was redeployed to the southwest Pacific, as were the five boats of 16th Squadron (Ron 16) which arrived to reinforce them as the fighting ended. A sixth boat, *PT-219*, was driven ashore and wrecked before she could be sent south. As the fighting moved on, the crews of the Higgins boats in Alaska might have been forgiven for appearing relieved that in future campaigns they would face the Japanese in a less hostile climate.

Above: An unidentified 80ft Elco boat entering Tulagi Harbor in late 1942. The island served as a forward base for PT boats during the campaign for control of the neighbouring island of Guadalcanal. (National Archives)

GUADALCANAL

During early summer of 1942 the Japanese occupied several islands in the Solomons Archipelago: New Ireland, New Britain, Bougainville, New Georgia, Shortland, Tulagi and several smaller islands. A major naval base was created on the island of Truk, where the remaining Japanese carrier fleet was based, and a forward naval base was established at Rabaul on the northern tip of New Britain. Despite the temporary setback caused by the Battle of the Coral Sea, the Japanese lay poised for further advances towards New Guinea and Guadalcanal. These would be the new battlegrounds in the Pacific. The Commander in Chief in the Pacific theatre, Admiral Chester W. Nimitz decided to take advantage of his victory at Midway by launching a 'limited' offensive against the Japanese in the eastern Solomons. The Japanese had already established a seaplane base on Tulagi, while engineers were building a forward airstrip on nearby Guadalcanal. Nimitz chose these island garrisons as his target. Ron 2 based in Panama was ordered to support the coming counter-offensive. The squadron's 14 boats were divided into two, with nine boats (PTs 37–39, 43–46, 48, 59–61) being redesignated as Ron 3 (the old designation of the 'expendable' Philippines squadron), while PTs 109–114 (all new 80ft Elco boats) were retained as Ron 2. The 2nd Squadron was commanded by Lt Rollin E. Westholm, while the 3rd Squadron was given to Lt-Cdr Alan R. Montgomery. Both formations were shipped to the southwest Pacific. The 4th Squadron remained a training squadron, so it was the 5th Squadron which replaced Ron 2 on the Panama station. On 7 August US Marines stormed ashore on both Tulagi and Guadalcanal, and while the smaller island fell in three days, the battle for Guadalcanal would continue into the new year, a struggle which sucked in troops, planes and ships like a whirlpool. It would become the crucial battle of the war, and the PT boats were ready to play their part. The 3rd Squadron arrived at Tulagi during October, and by early December the 2nd Squadron had joined them, bringing the PT-boat strength in the eastern Solomons up to 18 vessels. More were on their way.

As well as expecting reinforcements, the crews could also expect an improvement in the level of support they could expect. A new PT-boat base was established on the nearby island of Florida, which became the headquarters of the 1st Motor Torpedo Boat Flotilla, a new all-embracing PT-boat organisation in the South Pacific. Cdr Allen P. Calvert was appointed as its operational commander, while administrative command was given to Capt M. M. Dupre Junior, who held the post of Commander, MTB Squadrons, South Pacific. While Calvert directed operations, tactical control remained in the hands of the squadron commanders, Montgomery and Westholm. This new organisation put the PT boats on an established footing, and meant that rather than having to 'scrounge' supplies from other units, the boats and their crews were now supported by a dedicated logistical staff. The headquarters was soon renamed 'Calvertville', although the village of Sesapi, across the narrow channel on neighbouring Tulagi, where the tender *Jamestown* was moored, remained the main operational base for the boats themselves.

Montgomery's 3rd Squadron first saw action on 14 October, just the second night after the first four boats had arrived in the Solomons. A patrol led by Lt Montgomery in *PT-60* encountered two Japanese destroyers in 'Ironbottom Sound', the waters off Guadalcanal. The boat fired two torpedoes and scored two possible hits, but ran aground while making her escape and had to be rescued. *PT-48* also engaged the destroyers, but failed to hit anything with her single torpedo shot. It was the first time these boats had been used in their intended role, and their performance came as a disappointment to the crews, as it turned out that no hits had actually been made. Torpedo quality would soon become a major problem for the PT boat men, as it already was for American submariners, as many MkVIII 'fish' failed to explode on contact. Patrols of this type would be repeated every night throughout the Guadalcanal campaign as the Japanese used the 'Tokyo Express', using destroyers to bring in reinforcements and supplies down 'The Slot' of the Solomons chain under cover of darkness, while the USN tried to interdict these supply runs. During the hours of daylight, American aircraft could cover the area, and the PT-boat crews were able to rest and prepare for their next sortie. It was a hard, dangerous business, as the boats lacked radar, so night-time encounters often took place at point-blank range. Fortunately the only casualty was *PT-61*, whose bows were blown off by a Japanese shell. Through the skill of her crew she managed to limp back to Tulagi, where she was repaired. These encounters were commonplace, but although several Japanese ships were turned back and others were damaged, confirmed sinkings remained elusive. The situation improved in January 1943 when the 1st Flotilla began co-operating with PBY Catalina flying boats equipped with radar. This allowed the boats to be directed towards enemy ships, allowing the PT boats to find their prey with greater efficiency. Another threat to the Allied build-up on Guadalcanal was submarines, and the PT boat patrols were also charged with hunting down Japanese submarines operating in 'The Slot'. As torpedoes passed underneath their shallow hulls, they were virtually immune to such attack, and while they lacked the sonar equipment of destroyers, they

Below: Map of Guadalcanal showing the main PT boat area of operations. Note the route of the 'Tokyo Express'.

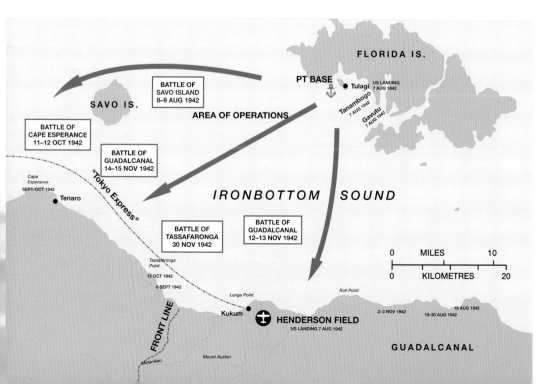

could attack an enemy contact quickly and efficiently with guns and depth charges. It was therefore appropriate that the first confirmed kill to a PT boat was a submarine rather than a surface warship. On the night of 9–10 December 1942, two PT boats were patrolling in Kamimbo Bay off Guadalcanal when they spotted a Japanese submarine on the surface, in the process of transferring stores onto a landing barge. Lt Robert L. Searles in *PT-59* fired two torpedoes at the boat, which was struck amidships. The Japanese submarine was later identified as the *I-3*, a Type 1 boat. Two nights later *PT-44* and *PT-110* ran into a force of three Japanese destroyers off Kolombangara Island near New Georgia. Outgunned, *PT-44* was riddled with gunfire and sank taking nine of her 11 crew with her, while the second boat made good her escape after sinking the 'Akizuki' class destroyer *Teruzuki* with her torpedoes, then disappearing amid the resulting confusion.

These engagements took place as a long and bitter battle was being fought in the waters and skies around Guadalcanal, as the Japanese troops on the island were gradually isolated and denied the supplies they needed. By January 1943 the lack of supplies had become critical for the Japanese, and the American drive around the landward flank of the Japanese army on the island began to gain momentum. On the night of 10–11 January the Japanese Navy launched a last-ditch attempt to run supplies through to the island, but forewarned, the PT boats were waiting for them. This time 13 PT boats were waiting for the Japanese destroyers, the force including the brand new 80ft Elco boats of Ron 6 (*PT-115–PT-126*), which had just arrived in the theatre under the command of Lt Clifton R. Maddux. In a vicious close-range night engagement three of the destroyers were torpedoed for the loss of two boats, *PT-43* and *PT-112*. Although the destroyers managed to limp away to safety, they had been thwarted in the attempt to run supplies through to the troops. Instead the destroyers dumped their cargo overboard in oil drums before they retired, hoping the drums would float ashore. Most never made it to the beach, and the following day the PT boats sank over 250 of them by gunfire. Denied the supplies they needed to continue the fight, the Japanese had no option but to withdraw their remaining troops. Consequently on the night of 1–2 February the Japanese Navy sent another 'Tokyo Express' destroyer flotilla, this time with orders to begin pulling off the troops. They were attacked by aircraft and surface vessels, then the PT boats were sent in. This time the fighting took place at daylight, which placed the 11 small vessels at a disadvantage, given the greater range and

Below: 34. An unidentified 77ft Elco boat on patrol near Lae, in New Guinea. The forward PT boat base at Morobe used native scouts to help crews navigate the local waterways of Morobe Province. (National Archives)

firepower of the Japanese guns. Worse, the American vessels were exposed to Japanese aircraft. *PT-37* exploded when her fuel tanks were hit, and *PT-111* and *PT-125* were wrecked by Japanese shells and bombs, and the near-suicidal attack was abandoned before further boats were lost. The only Japanese casualty was the destroyer *Makigumo*, which hit a mine as she was evading a torpedo attack. However, this vicious action helped to tighten the blockade around the island. There would be no Dunkirk-style withdrawal from Guadalcanal, and the few Japanese troops who escaped from the island did so in small groups, and at night. As the campaign ended the now fully blooded crews repaired and refitted their boats, and prepared for the next round of fighting in the Solomons. Meanwhile other PT boat squadrons were embroiled in a bitter fight with the Japanese further to the west, in the hard-fought campaign for New Guinea.

THE NEW GUINEA CAMPAIGN

New Guinea, the last island before the mainland of Australia was regarded by both sides as one of the most valuable prizes in the southwest Pacific. The Japanese began massing for an assault on the island at their new base on Rabaul, and the Australians requested help in defending the island. Four of the seven boats of Ron 1 which had avoided being sent to the Aleutians were duly sent south from Pearl Harbor in company with the MTB tender *Hilo*, the group having been redesignated Division 2 of the squadron, a detached formation under the command of Lt Jonathan F. Rice. His force consisted of *PT-21*, *PT-23*, *PT-25* and *PT-26*, as

Below: An unidentified Elco boat based on New Guinea in the southwest Pacific, where several squadrons supported the advance of American and Australian ground troops by intercepting Japanese supply convoys, and running supplies to their own troops along the northern coast of the island. (National Archives)

PT-20, *PT-29* and *PT-30* of Ron 1 remained in Pearl Harbor undergoing repairs. By early November 1942 Rice's force had reached the Gilbert and Ellice Islands, just over half way to its destination. By that time the situation in New Guinea had changed dramatically. On 21 July a Japanese invasion force had landed near Buna on the southeastern side of the island, and had begun an advance up the Kokoda trail towards the main Allied base at Port Moresby, on the far side of the island. The Australian troops in the area were driven back into the Owen Stanley Mountains, but in mid-September the Japanese advance was halted by veteran Australian troops, fresh from the desert of North Africa. Meanwhile a second Japanese landing had been made at Milne Bay, on the eastern tip of New Guinea. The Australian garrison held its ground, and on 7 September the battered Japanese force was withdrawn. Therefore by late September it was clear that the threat to Port Moresby was over, and Rice's boats would form part of an Allied counter-attack. This began in early November, and by the end of the month the Japanese were pinned against the coast around Buna by a

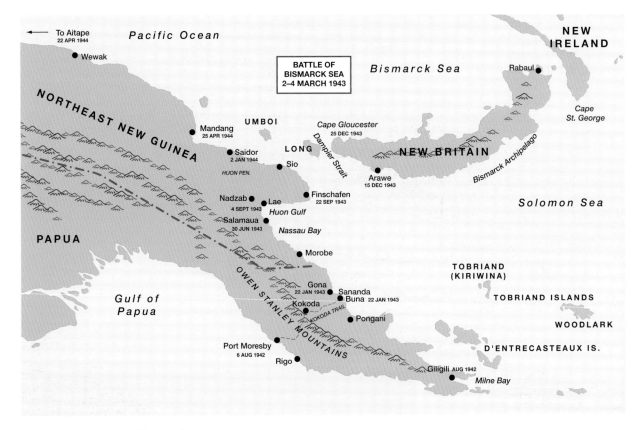

Above: New Guinea and Battle of the Bismarck Sea.

division each of Australian and American troops. The war, Lt Rice felt, was passing him by. Leaving the boats of Division 2 in the Ellice Islands, the MTB tender *Hilo* continued on to Cairns in Australia, where it rendezvoused with a new force, shipped directly from the US. This was a makeshift squadron of six boats commanded by Lt Daniel S. Baughtman; *PT-113*, *PT-114* and *PT-119–PT-122*. In September the first two boats had been transferred to the force (temporarily designated as part of Ron 2) from the 5th Squadron, while the remaining four boats formed part of the 6th Squadron. Together with the *Hilo* this composite force was soon ordered to establish a new forward PT boat base at the deserted Porlock Harbor, New Guinea, some 50 miles southeast of Buna. The boats arrived in mid-December, and made contact with the enemy on their first patrol. On the night of 18–19 December *PT-121* and *PT-122* engaged a surfaced Japanese submarine, but no torpedo hits were scored. However *PT-122* had a second chance five nights later, when she engaged and reportedly hit another submarine on the surface. Rather than sinking her, the submarine dived and fired back. The PT boat crew later claimed a kill against the *I-22*, which had already been lost in the waters of the Solomons. It must have been a confusing night. However, *PT-114* and *PT-121* had more luck off Buna, where they shot up Japanese barges moving troops along the coast. These attacks would become commonplace in the weeks which followed as the Buna campaign reached its bloody climax. By 3 January Japanese resistance in the area had been overcome, and the fighting shifted further north, first to Salamaua, and then towards the large Japanese base at Lae. This involved the interception of Japanese attempts to resupply these bases via the Bismarck Sea, and the prevention of nocturnal enemy troop movements along the coast using landing barges.

Reinforcements arrived in time to participate in the new campaign in late February 1943; 12 boats of Ron 7 (*PT-127–PT-138*) commanded by Congressional Medal of

Honor winner Lt-Cdr John D. Bulkeley, and seven of Ron 8 (*PT-66–PT-68, PT-142, PT-143, PT-149* and *PT-150*) under the command of Lt-Cdr Barry K. Atkins. With the exception of the 77ft Elco boats *PT-66–PT-68*, all these vessels were 80ft Elco boats. While Ron 7 was a new formation, Ron 8 consisted of *PT-66–PT-68* transferred from Ron 4 in addition to her four new boats. At this stage of the war Elco was producing 8–10 boats a month, and these vessels represented the latest PT boats to enter active service. Apart from Ron 6 which was sent to the Solomons, the only other new boats in service; *PT-103–PT-114*, formed Ron 5, stationed in Panama. Of these, *PT-109–PT-114* were reassigned to Ron 2, which itself was split into two divisions, one in the Solomons and the other, under Baughtman's command, fighting in New Guinea. The only New Guinea boats, *PT-110, PT-113* and *PT-114* arrived in time for the final attack on Buna. Ron 8 was to be reinforced by five more boats in January 1943 (*PT-144–PT-148*), but instead these were allocated to Ron 2 in New Guinea, and only *PT-143* was transferred to Atkins' command in June 1943. The other boats were reallocated to the newly formed Ron 12 on 1 June 1943, when Ron 2 was consolidated.

By 1 March the boats were operating in the Bismarck Sea itself, where a convoy of 16 Japanese supply and transport ships was sighted. It was attacked by B-17s, accounting for four destroyers and three transports. Stripped of many of its escorts, the convoy was now an easier target for the PT boats. On the night of 3–4 March *PT-143* and *PT-150* sank the damaged Japanese supply ship *Oigawa Maru*, and over the following days other boats engaged and destroyed smaller Japanese troop transport barges, causing a heavy loss of life, and preventing the reinforcement of the Japanese garrisons in New Guinea at Lae, Saidor and Madang. The boats of what was now dubbed 'MacArthur's Navy' were earning their keep. These patrols continued in the Huon Gulf and the Bismarck Sea through the spring and into the summer, while MacArthur prepared his troops for a fresh offensive.

Above: *PT-328*, an 80ft Elco boat, was attached to the 21st Squadron (MTB Ron 21), and served in the Pacific, where the squadron won a Presidential citation. She carries a 40mm gun on her quarterdeck, a 37mm gun forward, and two twin 0.50cal turrets amidships. The boat survived the war, and was sold out of service in 1946. (US Navy)

Transport barges and even submarines were frequently engaged, but the crews scored no dramatic successes over the enemy during this period. However, the crews now enjoyed a better level of support, as Task Group 70.1 was formed in March, which meant that the older operational formation — TG50.1 — was now part of the US 7th Fleet, attached to MacArthur's Command rather than the 1st Flotilla headquarters in the Solomons. Cdr Edgar T. Neale was given command of the flotilla, which included boats from three MTB squadrons. With improved logistical support, the boats could rely on a steady supply of torpedoes, spares and provisions, while ancillary vessels were made available to provide makeshift depot ships for the boats in their otherwise primitive forward bases. All this reorganisation was vital, as the small force of boats in New Guinea was being transformed into a major fleet. Task Group 70.1 would end the campaign the following year with just over 180 PT boats under its command. In the end, Ron 7 and Ron 8 would eventually be reinforced by 13 other squadrons.

In March, *PT-67* and *PT-119* were destroyed by an accidental fire whilst refuelling at Tufi, New Guinea, prompting the transfer of boats of Lt Baughtman's Division of Ron 2 to Ron 8 three weeks later, part of the tidying up when the boats became part of the 7th Fleet. On 1 June Ron 2's New Guinea Division was disbanded, and its remaining six boats (*PT-110*, *PT-144–PT-148*) were transferred to Ron 8 (*PT-110* and *PT-144*), and the new outfits Ron 12 (*PT-145*, *PT-146*), and Ron 18 (*PT-147*, *PT-148*).

Above: The 80ft Elco boat *PT-150* in the foreground participated in several attacks on Japanese submarines during the campaign in the southwest Pacific in 1942. She is shown here during a period of rest and maintenance off Amsterdam Island while serving in New Guinea. (US Navy)

These two new squadrons formed part of the first wave of reinforcements for 'MacArthur's Navy' brought in during the preparations for Operation 'Cartwheel'. Ron 12 was commissioned in February 1943, but officially entered service in June, Lt-Cdr John Harllee being appointed the 12th Squadron's first commanding officer. In addition to *PT-145* and *PT-146*, it consisted of the new 80ft Elco boats *PT-189–PT-196*, and *PT-150* transferred from Ron 8, giving it a strength of 11 boats. Ron 18, commanded by Lt-Cdr Henry M. Swift was formed around the 80ft Elco boats *PT-147* and *PT-148*, transferred from Ron 2 on 1 June. These boats were reinforced during the summer by six more 80ft Elco boats, *PT-362–PT-367*, and four 70ft Scott-Paine boats, originally built for service in the Dutch Navy, and now designated *PT-368–PT-371*. Thus when Operation 'Cartwheel' began, Task Group 70.1 had 35 boats at its disposal; 12 from Ron 7, 12 from Ron 8 and 11 from Ron 12. More were to arrive as the campaign unfolded, including the reinforcements sent in July and August to help form Ron 18.

Operation 'Cartwheel' was designed to clear the Japanese from lower New Guinea, allowing troops to cross over to New Britain and advance on Rabaul. This would clear the Solomon Sea basin of Japanese, and would allow MacArthur to threaten northern New

Guinea and the Admiralty Islands, both stepping stones on the way back to the Philippines. The operation began in June 1943 with an advance on Lae from Morobe, and later from Wau, in the New Guinea hinterland. The boats of Ron 8 played their part, transporting American infantry forward during the landings at Nassau Bay, and intercepting Japanese attempts to sneak reinforcements across the Huon Gulf.

An average of 12 Japanese transport barges were destroyed by the boats of Task Group 70.1 throughout the year, off Lae, Finschafen and other Japanese strongholds. Indeed, one Japanese soldier recorded that he had sailed in a barge convoy from New Britain to Finschafen

Above: *PT-68* berthed in New Guinea, 1943. She was a 77ft Elco boat which was originally given the peacetime designation *PTC-36*. She ran aground off Morobe in New Guinea in late September 1943, and had to be destroyed to prevent her capture. (US Naval Institute)

without being attacked by enemy PT boats, the first to make the crossing without incident. The waters off Cape Cretin became a happy hunting ground for the boats, and following the capture of Lae and Finschafen in September, the boats rounded Cape Cretin and operated in the Vitiaz Strait and Astrolabe Bay as far north as Saidor. While the Japanese army conducted a fighting retreat from the Huon Peninsula, the PT boats prevented any attempt to infiltrate back behind the advancing Allies. A force of 45 barges was destroyed off Morobe during an attempted landing behind the front line during November, and while the Allies continued to leapfrog up the coast, the PT boats followed on behind, engaging Japanese coastal barges to prevent the garrisons from being reinforced. The campaign was not fought without losses. During late 1943, *PT-68*, *PT-136*, *PT-147* and PT-322 were all wrecked when they ran aground, while the wear and tear on the older boats made it increasingly difficult to keep them in action. Still, any losses could be easily replaced. One new squadron arrived in the theatre every month during late 1943. Ron 21 was formed in April, Ron 24 in May and Ron 25 in June, and all entered active service during the period between September and November 1943. Ron 21 commanded by Lt-Cdr Selman S. Bowling consisted of the 80ft Elco boats *PT-320–PT-331*. Ron 24, commanded by Lt-Cdr Bert Davis was also made up of 80ft Elco boats (*PT-332–PT-343*), as was Ron 25, commanded by Lt Daniel S. Baughtman Jr., which contained *PT-344–PT-355*.

The offensive had slowed somewhat after the fall of Lae and the Huon Peninsula, but on 15 December US Marines landed at Arawe in New Britain, followed by a larger landing at Cape Gloucester at the western tip of the island 11 days later. In January 1944, leapfrog landings were made at Saidor (2 January) and Sio (15 January), and a month later marines cleared Rooke Island, which lay in the straits between New Guinea and New Britain. The Solomon Sea was slowly being cleared of the Japanese, and the PT boats were helping by supporting the landings, then interdicting the enemy coastal barge movements despite the appalling conditions, where the boats were often buffeted by monsoons and mini typhoons.

By this stage the boats had begun to operate a system where each unit commander (usually a division of 3–4 boats) would send in two reports each day to Task Group 70.1 headquarters, wherever it was that day. One would report the actions of the previous night, and the second would be an 'intent' message, outlining where the boats planned to operate the following night. At headquarters Cdr Bowling passed on these 'intent'

Above: The 80ft Elco boat *PT-362* served in the southwest Pacific as part of the 18th Squadron (MTB Ron 18) from late 1943 onwards. She survived the war, and was destroyed at Samar in late 1945. (US Naval Institute)

messages to all other relevant commanders, in an effort to reduce the risk of friendly fire, and to avoid multiplicity of effort. While boats rarely operated in full squadron strength, these larger formations still played a part during major operations, such as the support of a landing, or the transport of troops. The system worked well, but it did not prevent all unfortunate incidents of friendly fire.

As the boats began operating in close support of the landings they began suffering more casualties. On 7 March *PT-337* was sunk by Japanese shore batteries in Hansa Bay while probing the coast north of Madang, while three weeks later *PT-121* and *PT-353* were both sunk by a 'friendly fire' incident, when they were bombed by Australian aircraft in Bangula Bay, off the northern New Britain coast. Just over a month later a similar disaster occurred off Cape Pomas, halfway along the northern coast of New Britain, facing the Bismarck Sea. *PT-347* had run aground, and she was in the process of being pulled off the reef by *PT-350* when both boats were attacked by US Marine Corsairs. The boats fired back, shooting down one of the Corsairs and driving off its wingman, but an hour later more planes arrived, just as *PT-346* arrived on the scene to help. This time the attacking planes strafed and sank both *PT-346* and *PT-347*, losing one USN Hellcat in the process. In all the 25th Squadron lost 14 men killed and 13 injured, plus two boats that day, the worst day of losses suffered by the PT boats during the campaign. Allied aircraft had been enjoying air superiority over the Bismarck Sea during March 1944. By April it was clear that the campaign was drawing to a close in the southwest Pacific. By mid-March the Japanese were in full retreat on New Britain, pulling back to their fortified base at Rabaul. Madang fell in late April, bringing Operation 'Cartwheel' to a close.

While the battle for the perimeter of Rabaul was taking place during the first few months of 1944, with Allied advances in New Britain matched by landings in the Solomons chain as far as Bougainville, the Japanese could still bring in supplies by air and sea through the Bismarck Sea. The only way to seal off Rabaul completely was to land troops on the Admiralty Islands, the group situated northwest of the Japanese stronghold, guarding the northern fringe of the sea. On 29 March a 'reconnaissance in force' was launched against the islands when the US 1st Cavalry Division landed on Los Negros. While the initial landings were unopposed, Japanese resistance further inland proved tougher, and it was not until late March before the islands were cleared of the Japanese garrison. During this time the PT boats of Ron 18 and Ron 21 were brought up to provide close-in support for the troops. A base was established around the tender *Oyster Bay* anchored in Seeadler Harbor, but the boats and their crews were subjected to sniper fire from the shore for several days until the last Japanese resistance was overcome. Meanwhile they occupied themselves attacking enemy shore positions, some boats even employing light 60mm infantry mortars to boost their firepower. With the Admiralty Islands in American hands the encirclement of Rabaul was complete. The base would be by-passed, allowing MacArthur to concentrate on his drive on the Philippines. This would involve a continued campaign of leapfrogging up the coast of Dutch New Guinea, and while the two PT boat squadrons based in the Admiralty Islands would continue the siege of Rabaul, others would follow the advance up the New Guinea coast. Hollandia and Aitape would be captured in April, then Arare and Sausapor in May. By August the campaign for New Guinea proper would draw to a close, and the battle for the islands beyond would begin. This meant the Philippines.

PT boat losses continued during this period; *PT-136*, *PT-145*, *PT-193* and *PT-339* were all wrecked after running aground on uncharted reefs, while *PT-133* was destroyed by Japanese shore batteries off Cape Pus in July 1944. The final casualty of the campaign was *PT-363*, which was also sunk by shore batteries while probing Knoe Bay on Halmahera Island off the western tip of New Guinea on 25 November 1944. The ending of the campaign for New Guinea meant that the PT boat crews of 'MacArthur's Navy' were given a short respite while American forces prepared themselves for the assault on the Philippines, earmarked to take place in November 1944.

The boats had performed superbly during the New Guinea campaign, and would remain at the forefront of the fighting for the Philippines which followed, by which time their role as inshore multi-purpose gunboats was assured. In no theatre of war in the Pacific did the PT boats prove more useful than in the waters of New Guinea. Although they rarely used their torpedoes, they became true multi-purpose craft: gunboats, escorts, patrol craft and high-speed interceptors. They also acted as scouting craft, and even embarked friendly natives for the purpose of providing local knowledge as the boats probed the coasts and river estuaries of the area. The campaign proved a vital learning process for the crews, and gave these men the experience they needed to train fresh crews and squadrons as they arrived to join in the Allied advance. A similar campaign of close co-operation between PT boats and American land, sea and air units was also fought in the Solomons, with the result that by the middle of 1944, the USN's PT boat crews had become hardened fighters, well-versed in the skills required of them in the bitter island hopping which would take place in the last year of the war in the Pacific.

THE SOLOMONS

After the conquest of Guadalcanal, the next move was a drive up the chain of the Solomon Islands towards Bougainville, New Ireland and New Britain. This meant a series of 'island-hopping' landings, where the PT boats would operate much as they did in the waters of New Guinea. The PT boats of the 1st Flotilla had become veterans during the fight for Guadalcanal, and during the offensive which followed their crews would be able to provide experience for the reinforcements sent to join the flotilla. Lt Westholm's battered Ron 2 was down to just four boats; *PT-109*, *PT-110*, *PT-113* and *PT-114*. Lt-Cdr Montgomery's Ron 3 was stronger with eight boats; *PT-38*, *PT-39*, *PT-45*, *PT-46*, *PT-48* and *PT-59–PT-61*. By contrast Ron 6 commanded by Lt Maddux was almost at full strength with 11 boats, *PT-115–PT-124* and *PT-126*. While Ron 3 would be

Below: The main battles around the Solomons. Note 'The Slot'.

Above: The 80ft Elco boat *PT-107* participated in the Solomons Campaign in the South Pacific, but was lost through an accidental fire while alongside the dock at Emirau on 18 June 1944. (US Navy)

reinforced by two replacement 77ft boats in November 1943 (*PT-40* and *PT-47*), Ron 2 became a replacement pool for other squadrons, having lost part of its strength in New Guinea. *PT-113* and *PT-114* were transferred to Ron 8 in New Guinea on 1 April 1943, while *PT-110* would follow two months later. This left *PT-109*. For operational purposes she was be attached to Ron 3 during the Solomons campaign, and Ron 2 was be officially disbanded on 11 November 1943, to be reconstituted as a special force the following spring, operating in the English Channel.

Over the next few months, while the Japanese regrouped in the upper Solomons, the crews of Flotilla 1 also took advantage of the lull in the fighting by repairing their ships and amalgamating new drafts of men into their boats. By the time Guadalcanal fell most boats crews were down to minimal strength, as malaria, dengue and exhaustion took their toll. Sesapi and Calvertville were also subject to periodic air attacks, disrupting the normal operation of the flotilla, and denying the crews the peace they needed to patch up their boats. During this period Lt Westholm left *PT-109* and Ron 2 to become Calvert's new Operations Officer, so when the order came to help transport troops to occupy the Russell Islands in February, Ensign Larson was in command of the boat, a post he retained until a new commanding officer was assigned to the boat on 24 April; Lt (jg) John Fitzgerald Kennedy, USNR.

Additional patrols covered the familiar channels off Savo Island in case the Japanese returned to the Solomons. These operations became more difficult on 5 March, when a single plane dropped four bombs on Senapi, destroying the operations office and riddling the hull of *PT-118*. Then, on 7 April, the last major Japanese air strike in the Solomons managed to sink three Allied ships in Tulagi harbor and damage two others, temporarily disrupting MTB base operations. The Japanese might have been driven back, but their airforce based at Rabaul was just as big a threat as it had been during the fight for Guadalcanal, while the Japanese Navy was bloodied but unbowed.

Starting in late April, the boats began operational patrols around the Russell Islands and in June the offensive against the central Solomons began, timed to coincide with MacArthur's offensive in New Guinea. In fact, Operation 'Cartwheel' saw simultaneous advances in both theatres in the southwest Pacific. The first target was Rendova Island. Landings were made there on 30 June, the same day as MacArthur's men were storming ashore at Salamaua near Lae, and even more troops landed on New Georgia, an island which was heavily defended by the Japanese, and the site of Munda, their largest airfield in the central Solomons.

In early July a forward or 'bush' base was established on Rendova Island, centred on the island of Lumbari, on the northern fringe of the Rendova Harbor on the north side o

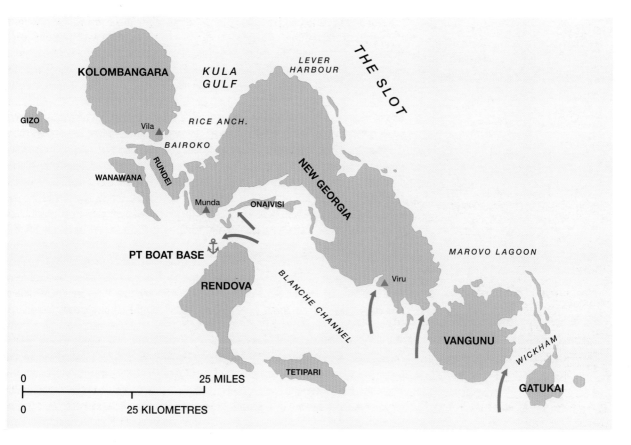

Above: Map showing the New Georgia landings. Japanese bases are shown in red. The Battle of Blackett Strait took place between Gizo and Kolombangara (see page 38).

the island. 'Todd City', named after the first PT-boat man killed during the New Guinea campaign, was an extremely rudimentary forward base, but it put the boats right at the heart of the fighting. The Japanese stronghold of Munda was just five miles away on New Georgia, on the far side of the Blackett Strait. The PT boats were back in the war. However, as the boats began offensive operations in the area, they were also placed in harm's way.

In late May, six boats were sent from Tulagi to reinforce the squadrons operating New Guinea. They sailed in company with the PT-boat tender *Niagara*, but on 23 May the force was attacked by Japanese aircraft. Although all the boats managed to survive the attack with only light damage, the precious tender was sunk, along with all its spare parts, supplies and ammunition. It would be months before the boats reached their new squadrons, and longer before the spare parts were replaced. Meanwhile, a freighter carrying reinforcements for the 1st Flotilla was torpedoed and sunk as it approached the Solomons, taking *PT-165* and *PT-173* down with her, as they were strapped to her decks. The other boats in the group (*PT-167*, *PT-171*, *PT-172* and *PT-174*) were being towed behind the freighter, and managed to escape the disaster. It looked as if the 1st Flotilla was being specially targeted by the Japanese, as the number of air attacks against boats and bases increased as soon as the PT boats moved forward from Tulagi to Rendova. After the war it was found out to be true; PT-boat patrols had proved so annoying that the boats were treated as a priority target by Japanese aviators. The reason was clear. Rendova lay on the southern tip of the cluster of islands which made up the New Georgia archipelago, itself located on the southern side of 'The Slot', or New Georgia Sound. Most of their islands were held by the Japanese, with principal enemy bases at Munda on New Georgia, and at Vila on neighbouring Kolombangara. To bring supplies

PT BASES
SOLOMON ISLANDS

Noumea, New Caledonia
Staging base where PT boats were
unloaded.
Opened: 9/42

Espiritu Santo, New Hebrides
Base 1, 2, 3, 15 where major engine
overhaul could take place.
Opened: 10/42

Tulagi
Base 1, 2, 8; Headquarters MTBSoPac
Opened: 12/10/42

Rendova
Base 11; Headquarters MTBSoPac
Opened: 30/6/43
Lever Harbor, New Georgia
Advanced base, shore-based operating
point
Opened: 24/7/43

Vella Lavella
Advanced base in Lambu Lambu Cove
Opened: 25/9/43

Treasury Islands
Base 9
Opened: 28/10/43

Cape Torokina, Bougainville
Base 9
Opened: 3/11/43

Green Island
Base 7, repair, supply, staging, training
Opened: 15/2/44

Homestead Lagoon
Base 16, shore-based operating point
Opened: 25/3/44

and reinforcements to these two bases, the Japanese had to traverse 'The Slot', then turn off into the Blackett Strait, or the Kola Gulf. While larger warships of the fleet patrolled the waters of 'The Slot', the PT boats were charged with intercepting Japanese barge movements into the Strait. Both sides realised just how important this stretch of water was.

The Japanese launched a major air attack against the PT boat base at Rendova on 1 August, appearing without warning as the boats were at anchor. Lumbari Island was hit by several bombs, while *PT-117* and *PT-164* were both destroyed before they could slip their moorings and roar off into the deeper waters of the bay. Although casualties were light, the crews were alarmed that their base was so vulnerable, despite the much-promised air cover of the USAAF. After all, two days before the crews had been given a dramatic illustration of just how effective this air cover was. On 30 July three PT boats were attacked by American B-25 bombers as they returned from patrol to Rendova. The planes mistook the boats for Japanese and launched an attack, and inevitably the PT-boat crews retaliated, shooting down one of the bombers. All three PT boats in the formation were hit, *PT-166* exploding, and the remaining two boats suffering casualties and light damage. Unfortunately the crew of the bomber were also killed, the victims of their own 'friendly fire' incident. Although extremely regrettable, these were tense times, and both boat and air crews were likely to fire first, then worry about recognition afterwards. Naval intelligence had just reported that the Japanese were planning a major 'Tokyo Express' mission to force through vital supplies and 1,000 reinforcements to Vila. These could then be ferried over to Munda. Without it, the base would fall to the Americans. What followed would be one of the biggest PT boat operations of the war, and one of the least successful.

Late in the afternoon of 1 August 1943, a group of five Japanese destroyers turned to starboard, out of 'The Slot' and into the passage between Kolombangara and Vella Lavella. The *Hagikaze*, *Arashi* and the *Shigure* were crammed with supplies, while the *Amagiri* provided the escort for the other destroyers. The 'Express' entered Blackett Sound after dark, and the PT boats were ready for them.

Some 15 PT boats were in the area that night; every available boat being sent from Rendova to intercept the Japanese destroyers. One division of five boats was held in reserve in the Ferguson Passage, between Gizo and Wana Wana, while the remaining ten were deployed in the Blackett Strait, directly in the path of the 'Tokyo Express'. These vessels were split into two divisions of five boats each, then further subdivided into groups of two to three craft, to improve the chances of encountering the enemy in the darkness. At least one boat in each division was equipped with radar, but these basic sets were of limited use in coastal waters. The most westerly group of PT boats included *PT-159*, which made radar contact around 10pm. Lt Brantingham thought the contacts were small barges, and roared forward to make an attack, forgetting to radio the other boats. The barges turned out to be destroyers, so Brantingham fired his torpedoes and turned away. The torpedoes missed, but they bought time for the PT boat to escape. He radioed for help and the other four boats of his division came to his aid, but in the dark missed the Japanese destroyers, who hugged the southern coast of Kolombangara to confuse the radar operators. Of the easterly division of PT boats, only *PT-171* made contact with the enemy, but scored no hits with its torpedoes, and the 'Express' reached Vila without any further incident around 12.30am. However, by the time they were ready to begin their return trip an hour later, the PT boats had regrouped, and were ready to bar their way again.

This time the most westerly group of boats, *PT-109*, *PT-162* and *PT-169* lay directly in the path of the Japanese destroyers. In her role as the escort vessel, the *Amagiri* was well in front of the others. Suddenly the crew of *PT-109* spotted a vessel approaching fast off their starboard bow. It was the Japanese destroyer. The range was too short to fire the torpedoes, so Lt Kennedy tried to pull his small boat out of the way. He was too late. The bow of the Japanese destroyer struck *PT-109* and cut her clean in two, then passed on into the night.

While John F. Kennedy and his men were struggling in the water, the rest of the group failed to hit the passing destroyers with their torpedoes. The same was true of the other PT boats further up the Strait. The Japanese slipped through unseen in the darkness, leaving their would-be ambushers with nothing to show for the loss of one boat and the expenditure of around 30 torpedoes but a dent in the bow of the *Amagiri*. Clearly large-scale PT boat operations were still poorly co-ordinated, as the crews lacked the experience of working together in large 'wolfpacks'. The 11 survivors of *PT-109*'s crew remained in the water throughout the night, and the following day they swam for the safety of a nearby island. Back in Rendova the crew were given up for dead, and it was only after a memorial service was held that

Above: The 80ft Elco boat *PT-166* on fire after a friendly fire incident off New Georgia on 20 July 1943, when the boat was attacked and destroyed by a flight of American B-25 bombers. (PT Boat Museum)

Kennedy managed to send word that he and his men were still alive, and waiting to be rescued. It was a dramatic finale to the story of *PT-109*, and an equally dramatic start to the public profile of the future president.

The PT boat action was overshadowed by a series of events which saw the Japanese lose control of central Solomons during the coming few months. First, Munda Airfield was captured on 5 August, although Japanese resistance on New Georgia continued for several weeks. The larger ships of the USN had been engaged in a series of encounter battles off the northern coast of New Georgia since early June, and during the night of 6–7 August they stopped a 'Tokyo Express' run, causing heavy casualties to the Japanese. The result was the Japanese abandoned further resupply convoys, and left the garrison on Kolombangara to its own devices. American planners decided to leave the island be, 'hopping' over it to land at Vella Lavella, then again on the Treasury Islands. On 1 November US Marines landed on Bougainville, and the following day the USN beat off a ferocious Japanese naval attack in the Battle of Empress Augusta Bay. From that point on, the waters of the Solomons were safe from Japanese warships, although coastal barges continued to move from island to island under cover of darkness. The PT boats were used to support the string of landings, and to seal off the islands skipped over by the advance.

However, while the Japanese Navy was no longer a threat, the air force based on Rabaul was still active. On 5 November *PT-167* was attacked off the coast of Bougainville, and one plane came in so low that it struck the PT boat's antenna and

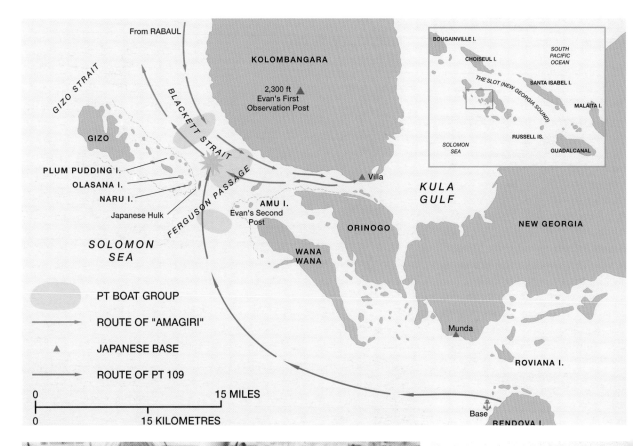

From RABAUL

KOLOMBANGARA

2,300 ft ▲
Evan's First
Observation Post

GIZO STRAIT

BLACKETT STRAIT

GIZO

PLUM PUDDING I.
OLASANA I.
NARU I.
Japanese Hulk

FERGUSON PASSAGE

Villa

KULA
GULF

AMU I.
Evan's Second
Post

ORINOGO

NEW GEORGIA

SOLOMON
SEA

WANA
WANA

BOUGAINVILLE I.

CHOISEUL I.

SOUTH
PACIFIC
OCEAN

SANTA ISABEL I.

THE SLOT (NEW GEORGIA SOUND)

MALAITA I.

RUSSELL IS.

SOLOMON
SEA

GUADALCANAL

PT BOAT GROUP

ROUTE OF "AMAGIRI"

▲ JAPANESE BASE

ROUTE OF PT 109

Munda ▲

ROVIANA I.

Base

RENDOVA I.

0		15 MILES
0		15 KILOMETRES

Top: The Battle of Blackett Strait took place on the
night of 1–2 August 1943.

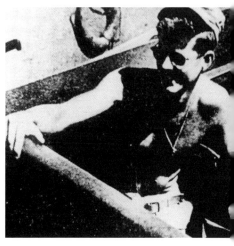

Above: Lt (jg) John F. Kennedy in the cockpit of his 80ft Elco boat, *PT-109*. The vessel formed part of the 2nd Squadron (MTB Ron 2) based at Rendova in the Solomons during 1943. (Library of Congress)

Left: The bridge of the 80ft Elco boat *PT-157*, pictured in the Solomons during late 1943. While under the command of Lt Liebenbow in early August, *PT-157* rescued Lt (jg) Kennedy and the stranded crew of *PT-109* off Patparan. (PT Boat Museum)

Left: The stern of *PT-109*, the Elco boat commanded by Lt (jg) John F. Kennedy. The photograph was taken during her shipment from Pearl Harbor to the South Pacific on board the transport ship S.S. *Joseph Stanton* in late 1942. (US Naval Institute)

Above: *PT-59* photographed at Tulagi in September 1943. The figure sitting in the boat's cockpit is John F. Kennedy. Note the addition of extra machine guns along the vessel's beam, each protected by a small steel mantlet. During this period the PT boats in the Solomons were engaged in regular engagements against Japanese shore defences, so the extra protection proved necessary. (US Navy)

Navy & Marine Corps Medal
Lt (jg) John Fitzgerald Kennedy

For heroism in the rescue of three men following the ramming and sinking of his motor torpedo boat while attempting a torpedo attack on a Japanese destroyer in the Solomon Islands area on the night of August 1–2, 1943. Lt. Kennedy, Capt. of the boat, directed the rescue of the crew and personally rescued three men, one of whom was seriously injured. During the following six days, he succeeded in getting his crew ashore, and after swimming many hours attempting to secure aid and food, finally effected the rescue of the men. His courage, endurance and excellent leadership contributed to the saving of several lives and was in keeping with the highest traditions of the United States Naval Service.

crashed into the sea! The crew then felt a jolt, but the ship seemed fine. It was only after the battle that they discovered they had been hit by a Japanese torpedo, which had passed clean through the bows of the PT boat without detonating.

The fighting in the Solomons dragged on into the spring of 1944, but by that stage the region had been relegated to a sideshow, as preparations were being made for the next move to encircle Rabaul. Reinforcements were brought forward to join the PT-boat force, but for the most part these were held back for use in new campaigns. Most of the boat crews were now veterans of this kind of nocturnal warfare, but accidents and losses still occurred during these mopping up operations. On the night of 11–12 February, the brand-new *PT-279* was rammed and sunk during a squall by another new boat, PT-282. Both 78ft Higgins boats were part of Ron 23, a new outfit commissioned the previous summer, and which reached the Solomons in time for the final thrust against Bougainville. Other new units to arrive during late 1943 and early 1944 included Ron 19 (*PT-235–PT-244*), Ron 20 (*PT-245–PT-254*), Ron 27 (*PT-356–PT-361, PT-372–PT-377*), Ron 28 (*PT-546–PT-551, PT-378–PT-383*), Ron 31 (*PT-453–PT-455, PT-462–PT-473*), Ron 32 (*PT-474–PT-485*) and Ron 33 (*PT-137, PT-138, PT-488–PT-497*). While most of these formations only passed through the Solomons on their way to other theatres such as New Guinea, the Marianas or the Philippines, a few boats and crews never made it out of the Solomons. During a barge-busting mission on the night of 25–26 February, *PT-251* was hit by shore batteries and blew up, killing her entire crew. Another boat on the same mission returned to base with an unexploded Japanese shell embedded in the warhead of one of her torpedoes. Three weeks later, on the night of 17–18 March, Japanese fire from the shore also caught *PT-283*, and she blew up. On the night of 5–6 May a group of boats were ambushed by the Japanese off Bougainville, and *PT-247* was hit and sunk by hidden shore batteries. Other losses were accidental rather than operational. In June *PT-63* and *PT-107* were destroyed by an accidental fire whilst refuelling in the Treasury Islands, and other boats were damaged but not lost when they ran aground.

However, by late May the campaign was all but over. The last major pockets of resistance on Bougainville had been overrun, although American troops would continue

Below: As the Allies advanced, the PT boat squadrons also moved forward, establishing forward bases close to enemy-held islands and hostile sea lanes. This base at Mindoro was used to support operations to recapture the rest of the archipelago of the Philippines during 1944–45. (PT Boat Museum)

to fight in that awful backwater until the end of the war. However, by May Japanese activity outside the confines of Rabaul had ceased. On 1 May 1944 the operational control of the PT boats in the Solomons was transferred to Task Group 30.3, under Capt Edward J. Morgan, the former administrative commander of the 1st Flotilla. The Task Group was part of Vice-Admiral William F. Halsey's Third Fleet, part of Admiral Nimitz's command. However, within a month the ownership of the boats changed again, as MacArthur rather than Nimitz gained control of the units in the Solomons theatre. As part of General MacArthur's Southwest Pacific Area, these PT boats were redesignated Task Group (TG) 70.8, becoming part of MacArthur's Seventh Fleet. Together with the boats of TG 70.1 which had fought in the waters of New Guinea, these boats would lead the way back into the Philippines.

THE PHILIPPINES

When General MacArthur reached Australia in March 1942, he declared of the Philippines, 'I shall return.' By mid-1944, he was ready to make good that promise. Allied forces under his command and under Admiral 'Bull' Halsey had cleared the Japanese from most of New Guinea and the Solomons, and had captured the Admiralty Islands, encircling the Japanese naval base at Rabaul. In the central Pacific, the US Fifth Fleet commanded by Admiral Spruance was also advancing, 'island hopping' from the Gilbert Islands to the Marshalls, then on to the Mariana Islands. While this latter theatre was not suitable for PT boats given the distances involved between the island groups, we have already seen how the boats were perfect for the campaigns fought by Halsey in the Solomons and MacArthur in New Guinea. They would also be in their element during MacArthur's return to the Philippines.

Below: The US landings as they retook the Philippines.

In July, MacArthur persuaded President Roosevelt that the Philippines would be the next Allied objective in the Pacific, and ambitious plans were drawn up for the amphibious landing of more than 200,000 troops on Leyte, supported by the warships of MacArthur's Seventh Fleet and the carriers of Halsey's Third Fleet. MacArthur realised the importance of PT boats in cutting off the Japanese-held islands from each other, so he included Cdr Selman S. Bowling in the planning of the operation. Bowling was the new Commander, MTB Squadrons, Seventh Fleet, a command which incorporated Task Groups 70.1 and 70.8 in one administrative command. However, until a foothold could be gained on the islands and a forward PT boat base established, the closest the bulk of this small boat armada could get to the landing beaches was Mios Woendi on the northwestern tip of New Guinea. This was considered too far for effective operations, so a small self-sufficient force was included in the amphibious landing force. When American troops began landing on Leyte on 20 October 1944, they were supported by a flotilla of 45 PT boats under the command of Lt-Cdr Robert Leeson. His force consisted entirely of 80ft Elco boats, the crews of which were mostly veterans of the New Guinea campaign. Ron 7 had nine boats (*PT-127–PT-132, PT-134, PT-137* and *PT-138*), while

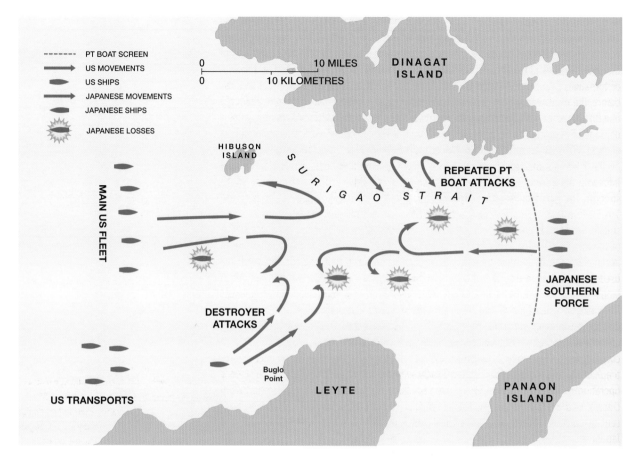

Above: The Battle of Surigao Strait, 24–25 October 1944.

another old New Guinea campaign formation, Ron 12, had 10 boats at its disposal (*PT-127*, *PT-146*, *PT-189–PT-192*, *PT-194–PT-196* and *PT-150*). Next came two newer formations, Ron 21 with 11 boats (*PT-320–PT-331*) and Ron 33 with 10 boats (*PT-488–PT-497*). Finally a division consisting of half of the newly-formed Ron 36 was included in the force, consisting of *PT-532–PT-536*. These boats were accompanied by the PT boat tenders *Half Moon* (originally designed as a seaplane tender), *Oyster Bay*, *Wachapreague* and *Willoughby*, all of which had previously served as support tenders in New Guinea or the Admiralty Islands. The first boats arrived off Leyte on the 21st, followed by the rest of the force two days later, and they immediately began offensive night-time patrols. Once again their targets were Japanese barges, bringing forward troops and supplies to help counter the American advance. However, the Japanese planned a far more dramatic response to the invasion.

They responded by ordering three naval forces to converge on Leyte. From the north, Admiral Ozawa's carriers would draw off Halsey's 3rd Fleet, leaving the way clear for Admiral Kurita's force to strike MacArthur's invasion force from the west, supported by Admiral Nishimura's southern force. While Ozawa succeeded in diverting some of Halsey's carriers, enough American planes were left to launch a powerful strike against Kurita's surface fleet. When the battleship *Musashi* was sunk, Kurita turned back to the west. This left Nishimura, whose fleet of battleships, cruisers and destroyers were entering the Surigao Strait from the south. Once through the strait, MacArthur's transport ships would be at their mercy. The surface warships of Admiral Kinkaid's 7th Fleet were placed in their way, the American line preceded by a screen of 39 PT boats, deployed in three boat sections. The Battle of the Surigao Strait opened just before 11pm on 25 October 1944, when the radar operators on the PT boats detected the approach of Nishimura's warships. The conditions were near perfect for the Japanese, with calm seas and moonlight, and they were able to detect the waiting line of boats before the Americans were able to attack. In the scrappy series of engagements which followed, several attacks were made and dozens of torpedoes fired, but just like the engagement in the Blackett Strait just over a year before, the results were hugely disappointing. Of the 34 torpedoes fired by the boats, only one hit was made — against the Japanese light cruiser *Abukuma*. In return the Japanese damaged five of the attacking boats; *PT-130*, *PT-152*, *PT-321*, *PT-490* and *PT-493*, and of these, *PT-493* later sank despite the best efforts of her crew. The only advantage gained by the PT boats that night was that Lt-Cdr Leeson was able to keep Admiral Kinkaid informed about the Japanese progress, and report fairly accurately on Nishimura's strength. The job of stopping the Japanese attack fell to the larger surface warships of the 7th Fleet, a task they performed with singular success, sinking two battleships and two smaller warships in return for the loss of one American destroyer. Even that was the victim of friendly fire. The PT-boat crews had shown great bravery, but they seemed unable to achieve any results working together in large groups. From that point on, the boats were used in their less glamorous role, interdicting Japanese maritime supplies, escorting landing craft, landing small groups of troops and shooting up Japanese coastal targets. Another new type of enemy was the new Japanese suicide boats which began to appear. During the landing operation on Mindoro in mid-December, PT boats commanded by Lt-Cdr Fargo screened the landing beaches from attacks by these deadly vessels, and from conventional enemy warships; the only American force capable of protecting the amphibious craft from all the types of Japanese vessels facing them. During the Mindoro operation *PT-223* scored one of the most spectacular MTB successes of the war. On 26 December the boat, commanded by Lt (jg) Harry E. Griffin was part of a two-boat force sent to harry Rear-Admiral Kimura's task force near Mindoro when it encountered the Japanese destroyer *Kiyoshimo*. While the Japanese targeted *PT-221*, Griffin in *PT-223* fired two torpedoes, and sank the 2,100-ton destroyer.

Below: The bow of an unidentified 80ft Elco boat, as her crew prepare to come alongside a USN destroyer-escort, somewhere in the Pacific theatre, 1944–45. The larger Cannon ('Det') Class vessel is possibly acting as a makeshift temporary tender. (National Archives)

In January MacArthur turned his attention to Luzon, the main island in the Philippine archipelago. The landing in Lingayen Gulf was largely unopposed, as the Japanese sought to avoid the American naval guns by fortifying a line well inland from the coast. This left the PT boats with no direct role, save patrolling the waters of the archipelago, and trying to intercept Japanese movement by sea. However, Manila Bay was completely accessible, and this gave the boats a new purpose, isolating the Japanese garrison on the fortress island of Corregidor from the mainland. By February MacArthur was ready to attack the island directly, sending paratroopers to secure a foothold on the rock, then reinforcing them by amphibious assault. Intelligence placed the garrison at 6,000 men, but fortunately for the assaulting troops the true figure was less than 1,000 men. Although the parachute drop was a success and took the defenders by surprise, many of the parachutists missed the small landing zone and dropped into the sea. A group of PT boats were on hand to rescue them, and this they did, despite coming under heavy fire from the Japanese troops on Corregidor. The crew of *PT-376* even launched their rubber dinghy to rescue paratroopers stranded on the rocks at the foot of Corregidor's cliffs, all the while taking fire from the defenders directly above them. The island was a labyrinth of tunnels and underground chambers, and it took the Americans 12 days to subdue the Japanese. While this great fight was taking place the PT boats circled the islands, stopping Japanese attempts to swim to the safety of the mainland, or to infiltrate reinforcements from the shore. Finally the island was declared secure, and on 2 March 1945, *PT-373* carried General MacArthur back to his former headquarters on Corregidor, a week short of three years after he left the island on board John Bulkeley's *PT-41*. The general had returned.

With that dramatic conclusion to the campaign the battle for the Philippines

was all but over, although the fighting would continue against sporadic pockets of Japanese resistance until the end of the war. Even Corregidor was not completely free of the enemy, as the last Japanese troops finally came out of hiding there as late as 1 January 1946! During this mopping up period the battered PT boats continued their patrols, and fought their own private war against the Japanese. During this period nests of suicide boats were discovered and destroyed, while as late as mid-May PT-335 and PT-343 came across a fuel-starved group of six Japanese MTBs, which were duly sunk. Attacks from Japanese (and American) planes would continue into the spring of 1945, as would the possibility of shore fire from hidden Japanese positions. Of the 45 PT boats which formed the original MTB force in the Philippines, four were lost during the campaign. PT-493 of Ron 33 was lost in the Battle of the Surigao Strait on 25 October, while three boats of Ron 21 — PT-320, PT-321 and PT-323 — were either sunk or forced aground by Japanese air attacks off Leyte during early November. Indeed, PT-323 became the victim of a Japanese Kamikaze attack, the only PT boat lost in this way during the war. Despite the failure of the boats to take on Japanese warships in a stand-up fight, the boats proved extremely useful in their new role of patrol craft and barge-busters. Without them MacArthur might well have taken much longer to reconquer the Philippines, and victory would probably have been bought at a far greater cost.

Above: The 80ft Elco boat PT-579 entered service during the closing months of the war, and was assigned to the Pacific, where she formed part of the 39th Squadron (MTB Ron 39). Her armament included a 40mm Bofors in the stern, several 20mm guns and a Mk 50 rocket launcher on either side of her bridge. She was fitted with depth charges rather than torpedoes. (US Navy)

THE MEDITERRANEAN

Following the entry of the United States into the war in December 1941, a commitment was made to send ground troops to Europe. These men first saw action in early November 1942 during Operation 'Torch', when American troops landed in French-held North Africa. Together with the British they advanced east towards Tunisia, where they linked up with General Montgomery's British Eighth Army. This trapped the Axis army in Tunisia, and during the hard-fought campaign which followed the Allies tightened their grip on this last enemy foothold on the African continent. The first PT boats arrived in the theatre in late April 1943, when two US oilers berthed in Gibraltar and unloaded eight 78ft Higgins boats. These vessels formed the core of Ron 15, a formation set up in January

Opposite Above: On 2 March 1945 General MacArthur returned to the island fortress of Corregidor on board PT-373, three years after leaving the island on board PT-41. (US Navy)

Opposite Below: Following the recapture of the Philippines, most of the PT boat squadrons in the Pacific theatre were gathered together for repairs, where they awaited redeployment. These boats were docked at Leyte. (National Archives)

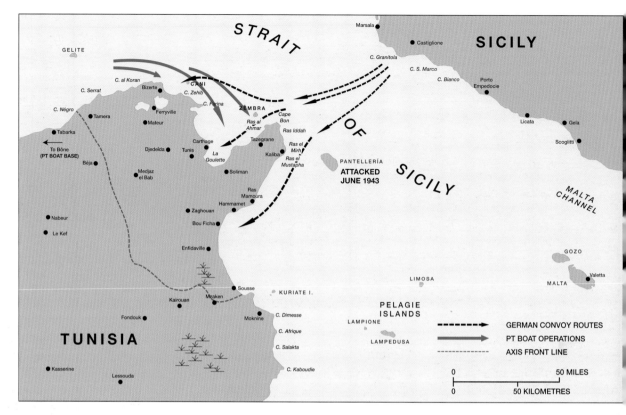

Above: PT boat operations against Axis resupply and convoy routes during the Tunisian campaign.

1943, under the command of Lt-Cdr Stanley M. Barnes, and consisted of *PT-201–PT-208*. Four additional boats, *PT-209–PT-212* were also on their way to Gibraltar, while another six boats, *PT-213–PT-218* would soon be sent to the Mediterranean as reinforcements, bringing the strength of Ron 15 up to 18 boats. Barnes led the first wave eastwards to the Tunisian port of Bône, the base used by British Inshore Forces, which would become Ron 15's parent organisation. British Coastal Forces had been operating in the Mediterranean since the war began three and a half years earlier, and they were therefore somewhat dubious about the combat effectiveness of these newcomers. However, any doubts about the capabilities of the American crews were soon dispelled. Ron 15 made its first combat patrol off Bizerte on the night of 25–26 April as part of the operation to interdict Axis attempts to escape by sea from Tunisia to the safety of Sicily or the Italian mainland. However, the first contact with the enemy came almost two weeks later, during the dark moonless night of 8–9 May. In a confused action in Ras Idda Bay near Bizerta, Barnes in *PT-206* fired a torpedo at a large target, and then came under fire from two British boats as he made his escape. Fortunately nobody was hurt. Meanwhile on the south *PT-203* picked up the crews of two British MTBs which had run aground while engaging another enemy vessel in shallow water. The American boat made good its escape, despite the lively fire from the shore.

That first taste of action set the scene for what was to follow; problems co-operating with an ally who used different methods, and the confusion inherent in operations off an enemy-held coast at night. However, Ron 15 had achieved its first success, and the squadron's British allies began to appreciate the enthusiasm of their new allies. However there were teething problems in the level of co-operation and communication between the two allies. Two nights later *PT-202, PT-204* and *PT-205* came under fire from a formation of British destroyers, who thought they were German E-boats. The mistake was understandable, as the German boats were attacking the British ships at the time. The PT

Above: 80ft Elco boats of the 29th Squadron (MTB Ron 29) pictured at their berths outside the inner harbour of Bastia in Corsica during late 1944. A squadron of British torpedo boats are seen behind them, alongside the sea wall. (US Naval Historical Center)

Left: Lt Douglas Fairbanks Junior halted his swashbuckling film career to become a real-life sea dog. Here he is seen aboard *PT-303*, a 78ft Higgins boat which served in the Mediterranean theatre. The photograph was taken during operations in the Adriatic, off the island of Vis. (PT Boat Museum)

Above: Operations in Central Italy and the Tyrrhenian Sea in 1943–44.

boats became embroiled in the engagement, taking fire from both sides until the Germans were driven off. On 13 May the Germans and Italians who remained in Tunisia surrendered to the Allies, and the squadron was able to repair its boats, and to integrate reinforcements, which brought the squadron strength up to 18 boats. It also gave a chance to iron out the communication problems with the British, before the next round of fighting began. Given that Ron 15 had been thrown into action with little consultation with the British, it is surprising the friendly fire incidents were not more plentiful. However, co-operation was now seen as important in future operations, and Barnes forged links with the command of British Inshore Forces. His squadron was also moved forward to Bizerta, just 100 miles from the coast of enemy-occupied Sicily.

In addition to attacking enemy coastal convoys, the PT boats were also used to land Office of Strategic Services (OSS) agents or reconnaissance parties on the Sicilian coast, in preparation for the Allied invasion. Often the boats were specially adapted for this role, with extra fuel tanks fitted, and extra rubber dinghies strapped to the deck. The build-up to the invasion of Sicily gathered pace during the next few weeks. On 11 June, the boats of Ron 15 participated in the invasion of Pantelleria, a small island halfway between Tunisia and Sicily, the only casualties to the force being one sailor killed during a German air attack against *PT-203*. A month later, it was the real thing: Operation 'Husky', the Allied invasion of Sicily, and the largest amphibious operation of the war so far. The small force of American PT boats would play its part in the great enterprise, first by guarding the port side of the invasion fleet as it steamed into position, and then on the morning of 10 July they acted as decoys, pretending to be landing craft and making dummy runs

at beaches far from the west of the beaches where the troops were actually landing. A handful of boats remained with the fleet during this period, serving as air-sea rescue boats, charged with rescuing downed pilots while the Allied air force covered the landing beaches. Four days later, on 14 July the squadron was ordered east, with orders to work with British Coastal Forces in sealing off Sicily from the Italian mainland. Although no contacts were made in the American sector, the overall small boat operation was a success, and the Axis defenders on the island were effectively cut off from reinforcements and supplies.

On 23 July Patton's troops captured Palermo, on Sicily's northern coast, and the squadron was moved there, where a forward PT boat base was established. The first night the boats operated night-time patrols from the new base was on the night of 24–25 July, when *PT-216* torpedoed and sank the Italian merchantman *Viminale* together with the tug which was towing her to safety up the Calabrian coast. This was the first of many operations against Axis coastal shipping, and unlike the actions fought against the Japanese, the Germans convoys consisted of large vessels worthy of torpedoes, and their escorts were exceptionally well armed. Two nights later the boats of Ron 15 were patrolling off the volcanic island of Stromboli when they ran into a well-armed convoy consisting of three 'F-Lighters', a type of well-armed barge (usually converted from prewar car ferries), and known by the Germans as *Marinefahrprahmen*. Six torpedoes were fired, but despite two explosions, no German vessels were sunk. As in many torpedo attacks of the war, faulty detonators or magnetic proximity devices caused the weapons to explode prematurely, or not detonate at all. Two nights after that, on the night of

Above: The 78ft Higgins boat *PT-211* pictured alongside the wharf in Bastia, Corsica, during late 1944. She has been fitted with makeshift rocket launchers on her quarterdeck, designed to be fired in support of amphibious landings. (US Navy)

FRANCE

• Valence

• Avignon

Milan •

Venice • Trieste •

Genoa
• Savona • Sestri Levante

Monaco • Porto Maurizio • La Spezia
Nice • San Remo
Cannes •
Marseilles • Toulon

LIGURIAN SEA

Rimini •

Florence •

Pisa •

ADRIATIC

ITALY

1944–45

1943–45 Calvi
Bastia •
CORSICA
Ajaccio•

Livorno •

ELBA
1943–45

Rome •

STRAIT OF BONIFACO 1943–44

Anzio •
Gaeta •

Bari •

Naples •
1944
Salerno •
CAPRI

SARDINIA

TYRRHENIAN SEA

Cagliari •

USTICA

LIPARI IS.

PT BOAT BASE (date in use)

MAIN GERMAN NAVAL BASES

MEDITERRANEAN SEA

Palermo •
Cape Granitola •
Porto Empedocle •

Messina •
STRAIT OF MESSINA
SICILY
Catania •

1943
Bizerte

1943
Bône •

Bougie •

ALGERIA

MALTA
1943

Sfax •

TUNISIA

50

Opposite: Overview of PT boat bases and the main German naval bases in the Mediterranean. See also box page 59.

Left: After the recapture of Corsica and Sardinia, the northern Corsican port of Bastia served as a base for British and American coastal forces. Here, 78ft Higgins boats of MTB Ron 15 are shown in the port's inner harbour, late 1944. (US Naval Historical Center)

28–29 July a patrol of three PT boats ran into three Italian MAS boats, their own form of MTB. Rather wastefully the Americans fired torpedoes which passed under the Italian boats, and in the firefight which followed *PT-218* was badly damaged, but managed to limp home to Palermo the following morning. The PT-boat squadron in the Mediterranean was experiencing an intensity of action far greater than that usually experienced in the Pacific, reflecting the greater emphasis placed by the Germans and Italians on coastal warfare compared to the Japanese. The less-experienced American crews were also forced to learn the hard way, developing tactics and experimenting with different weapons as they went along.

In early September the squadron played its part in Operation 'Avalanche', the Allied landing at Salerno, on the Italian mainland. The invasion took place on 9 September, just hours before the Italian government had signed an armistice, removing its forces from the war. Nobody knew quite what to expect, except that the Germans would fight on alone, and would take over whatever Italian warships and equipment they could in the days following the Italian surrender. The landing was a costly success. The Allied troops were quickly trapped by the Germans in a vast mountain-ringed amphitheatre, but while these forces prevented the Allies from expanding the beachhead, other Allied forces crossed from Sicily to Calabria and Umbria, then advanced northwards. After three weeks the German ring around Salerno was broken, and the Germans retreated north through Naples to establish a new defensive line running directly across the Italian peninsula, passing through Cassino. The PT boats helped the armies by guarding the Salerno beachhead from attack, and escorting convoys containing reinforcements during the voyage from between Sicily to Salerno. All the boats of Ron 15 survived the battle, and *PT-211* was even credited with shooting down a German aircraft. During late 1943, new forward PT boat and MTB bases were established at Maddalena in northern Sardinia, and at Bastia in northern Corsica. Facilities in both ports were shared jointly by both the American PT boats and their British counterparts. The now experienced crews of Ron 15 were told they were to be joined by two more squadrons during this period, although the boats did not arrive in the combat area until late April 1944. For the moment, Ron 15 was on its own, and it was slowly becoming a useful part of the Allied naval operation in the Tyrrhenian and Ligurian seas. On the night of 22–23 October three PT boats intercepted a small but heavily escorted German convoy off Giglio and sank an enemy tanker of 4,000 tons. For the Germans, whose war machine in Italy was being starved of fuel, the loss was a serious one, achieved at the price of minor damage to *PT-207*. Although other boats were shot up or damaged during these patrols, none of the Higgins boats was lost.

Unlike the British MTBs and MGBs in Corsica and Sardinia, many of the American boats were fitted with radar. This led to the development of joint patrols, where a group of British boats would patrol off the Italian coast in search of a German coastal convoy, and the American boat would give the force advanced warning of any German movements. Lt-Cdr Barnes pioneered the scheme, and it proved such a success that it became standard operating procedure for the boats for the remainder of the war in the Mediterranean. This new arrangement was doubly important for the Allies, as from December 1943 on the Germans started using former Italian destroyers and destroyer escorts to protect their coastal convoys, giving them a firepower which the frail PT boats and British Coastal Forces craft were hard-pressed to match. Their only real advantage lay in radar, and in the element of surprise. Three times during December the boats clashed with German destroyers off Corsica and Elba, but despite almost all boats firing their torpedoes, no German warship was even hit, let alone damaged. By spring 1944 the Allies had devised their own antidote to the well-armed F-lighters used by the Germans. This was a converted gunboat, adapted from a landing craft and armed with a pair of 4.7in guns, the weapon used on British destroyers. These formed the basis of a new type of Allied 'battle group', built around the gunboat (or LCG). The craft was escorted by around three British MTBs to protect the LCG from German E-boats while the main force was

Below: The 80ft Elco boat *PT-558* was originally designated *PT-55* in the Soviet Navy, but she was transferred to US naval service before delivery, and reclassified when she entered service in May 1943. She served in the Mediterranean theatre as part of the 29th Squadron (MTB Ron 29) until the end of the war. (US Naval Institute)

escorted by two groups, each of two PT boats. Both contained one boat fitted with radar. While one group served as a scouting force and radar picket, the second pair of boats became the control centre for the small squadron. The idea came from Cdr Allan of the Royal Navy, who adopted *PT-218* as his 'flagship'. A similar attempt was made to marry PT boats with destroyers, but the larger vessels proved too awkward for coastal warfare, and attracted the attention of shore batteries while driving away enemy shipping. The attempt was abandoned in favour of the Anglo-American Allan's 'battle group' which first went into action in late March. However, while this idea was being developed, the land campaign in Italy was gathering pace, and the PT boats were called away from their own private war to take part in a far larger operation.

During late January the boats were ordered to protect the Allied landings at Anzio. The first troops went ashore on 22 January, followed later that morning by General Clark, who used a PT boat to ferry him to the beachhead before being transferred to a landing craft for the final run ashore. He enjoyed the experience so much he ordered two PT boats to be made available to him for the next three months, so they could ferry him and his staff between Naples and the Anzio beachhead. The rest of the boats were used in a more conventional manner, protecting the landing ships and rescuing downed pilots. The lack of progress from the beachhead at Anzio meant that many of the boats remained there until late March 1944, when they were allowed to rejoin the campaign to intercept German coastal convoys. By that time the new hunting group had already seen action, far up the coast from Anzio, off the Tuscan coast. On the night of 27–28 March the group engaged a well-protected coastal convoy. While the MTBs and PT boats fired torpedoes at two destroyers to drive them off, the LGC gunboat shot up the rest of the convoy, sinking six F-Lighters. It was a signal success, repeated a month later on 24–25 April when the group sank five F-Lighters, the total including two sunk by PT boats, most probably *PT-202* and *PT-213*. The system worked like a charm.

Above: During a patrol off the northern Italian port of Genoa, the 78ft Higgins boat *PT-204* was damaged when she rammed a German minesweeper. She was taken back to Bastia for repairs. Note the rocket launcher mounted on her forecastle. (US Naval Historical Center)

Above: During the amphibious landings at Salerno in Italy in September 1973, PT boats helped protect the invasion fleet, and patrolled the landing site in the weeks following the invasion. Here two 78ft Higgins boats are seen with a tank landing vessel (LST) in the background. (US Navy)

Just as this system was proving its worth, the long-promised reinforcements arrived in Bastia. Like Ron 15, Ron 22 was equipped with 78ft Higgins boats, *PT-302–PT-313*. These 12 new boats arrived in the Mediterranean in November, just days after the arrival of a squadron of 80ft Elco boats, designated Ron 29. These vessels, *PT-552–PT-563*, had all been built with the intention of supplying them to the Soviet Navy as part of the Lend-Lease programme. However, for operational reasons they were transferred to the USN in May 1943, formed into a PT boat squadron, then shipped out to the Mediterranean. These 12 boats were the only Elco boats to serve in the European Theatre of Operations until just before D-Day in June 1944, when two squadrons of 80ft boats arrived in Britain. One unusual feature of the Ron 29 boats was that several of them were fitted with the Thunderbolt, a six-barrelled 20mm gun mounting which provided the boats with a phenomenal level of firepower at short range. Ron 22 was commanded by Lt-Cdr Richard J. Dressling, while Lt-Cdr S. Stephen Daunis was in charge of Ron 29. These new crews arrived after the Salerno operation and spent a few months in the Naples area in case they were needed somewhere other than the Ligurian Sea, where the Bastia-based boats were patrolling. Therefore they missed the early successes of Ron 15 but arrived in time for the Allied breakout from the Anzio and Cassino positions, and the drive northwards through Rome into Tuscany. While Ron 22 was sent to Bastia to join Ron 15, Ron 29 was based further down the Corsican coast at Calvi, facing the southern coast of France. The reason for this deployment would soon become clear, but the crews suspected the reason when they were ordered to train alongside landing craft. Clearly Ron 29 was destined to play a part in any coming invasion of southern France. With three PT boat squadrons in the theatre, the Eighth Fleet now had a powerful new weapon, and needed a commander to take charge of it. Lt-Cdr Barnes was named as Commander, Boat Squadrons, Eighth Fleet, a post he held in addition to running Ron 15, which was now divided between Bastia and Calvi. With the two ports filled with American and British boats, landing craft, small warships and supply vessels, it was clear that the naval war was about to enter a new phase.

While the raids on German coastal convoys continued, the attacks spearheaded by Cdr Allan's battle group, plans were laid for a new amphibious operation, this time against the island of Elba. The operation was considered important to protect the seaward flank of the Allied armies as they advanced north, although with hindsight the island might well have been left to 'wither on the vine' as so many Japanese bases were in the Pacific. Instead, all available boats were pressed into service for the operation, codenamed Operation 'Brassard'. Some served as troop transports, some as escorts, and others as rocket-armed gunfire support craft. The assault troops from the French 9th Colonial Division supported by British and French Commandos landed from landing craft, PT boats and British MTBs on the night of 17–18 June, and despite initially heavy resistance and the loss of several landing craft, the island was captured. During that

Below: A 78ft Higgins boat coming alongside a friendly vessel off Salerno, September 1943. Her zebra pattern camouflage scheme was designed to confuse the enemy over the size of vessel they were looking at, and her direction of travel. The scheme was used in a limited way in both the Mediterranean and the Pacific theatres. (National Archives)

Above: 80ft Elco boats of the 34th and 35th Squadrons (MTB Ron 34 and 35) photographed in the weeks before D-Day in the harbour of Portland on the English south coast. The base served as a munitions centre, where PT boats were resupplied with torpedoes and ordnance. (US Navy)

confused night the Allied boats found themselves thrust into a bitterly-fought action against a German naval group, an action initiated by accident. In the darkness *PT-210* came alongside a vessel it thought was part of the landing force. It turned out to be a German Flak lighter, and *PT-210* was lucky to survive the resulting exchange of point-blank fire before the two ships parted. Although several boats were damaged in similar clashes that night, somehow all the PT boats survived the operation, the baptism of fire for two out of the three American squadrons who took part in the invasion. This served them in good stead two months later, when the boats were called upon to actually land troops on the shore of France, as part of Operation 'Anvil'. As landing craft were in short supply, Barnes's flotilla was ordered to act as makeshift landing boats, and on 15 August some 30 boats were involved in the operation, many of them landing hundreds of American and French troops by rubber dinghies on the coast between Cannes and Porquerolles Island, on the French Riviera. Corsica served as the staging area for the operation, and for a few weeks Calvi became one of the most bustling ports in Europe. During the landing operation other PT boats and British coastal vessels protected the landing sites from attack, and boats from Ron 29 helped sink two German escort vessels from Toulon who tried to attack the landing ships. Although the landing was a success, and both Toulon and Marseilles were in Allied hands within two weeks, the flotilla suffered its first losses in almost a year of combat operations. On 16 August *PT-202* hit a mine in the Gulf of Fréjus near St. Tropez and sank, as did *PT-218* which came to her aid. Just over a week later *PT-555* also hit a mine, and sank as she was being towed back to Calvi.

In the months which followed the boats continued to operate off what was increasingly becoming a friendly coast. While operations were winding down, and many British coastal forces boats were transferred to the Adriatic, the American PT boat squadrons were also beginning to scale down their operations. Offensive patrols still operated off the northern Italian coastline of the Ligurian Sea, and on the night of 13–14 September *PT-559* even torpedoed and sank a German escort vessel during an attack on a convoy off Genoa. However, it was clear that the Mediterranean was gradually becoming a backwater, as the fighting moved north. On 17 October the veteran Ron 15 was decommissioned in Valletta Harbour in Malta, and the boats transferred to the Royal Navy. They promptly recrewed them and sent them around Italy to operate off the Yugoslavian coast, while the American sailors were shipped home, where they would be given new boats and sent to fight in the Pacific. The bases on Corsica were abandoned in favour of St. Maxime near Toulon, and then in October the final PT-boat base in the Mediterranean was established at Livorno (Leghorn). A final vessel would be lost off the port on 18 November, when *PT-311* struck a floating mine as she returned from a patrol. The Germans still held onto the north Italian plains until the final weeks of the war, and with it the ports of La Spezia and Genoa, both of which had been major Italian naval bases. These ports became the focus of Cdr Barnes's PT boats during the last months of the war, and patrols would continue until the liberation of Genoa by Italian partisans in late April 1945.

During the two years that American PT boats fought alongside the British Royal Navy in the Mediterranean, they reportedly sank some 23,700 tons of enemy shipping, mainly well-armed coastal barges, plus a handful of German and former Italian warships. This total excludes vessels sunk as part of joint operations with the British, where honours were rightly shared. This would add a further 15 enemy ships and 13,000 tons to the total. American losses were four boats sunk, and 24 sailors killed. The achievements of Cdr Barnes's PT boats were probably more spectacular than those of the PT boats in the Pacific, as they tended to operate in the role for which they had been designed. They sought out the enemy and sunk their ships using torpedoes as well as deck guns, and despite the faults of American torpedoes which continued to plague the war effort, they sank more enemy ships by torpedo than in any other theatre of operations. The Mediterranean saw PT boats at their best, operating as true hunters of the night.

THE ENGLISH CHANNEL

The PT boats came late to the war in the waters off enemy-occupied France, and they operated in a way which was unique in the annals of PT-boat warfare. On 11 November 1942 the USN decommissioned Ron 2, the outfit which had served in defence of Hawaii and Midway, before being shipped across the Pacific to New Guinea. In late March 1944 the USN reconstituted the squadron, but this time it would consist of just three boats. *PT-71*, *PT-72* and *PT-199* were all 78ft Higgins boats, two being built in July 1942 and *PT-199* in January 1943. Until the reformed Ron 2 was created, the boats served as training vessels, attached to the PT Boat Training Center at Melville, Rhode Island. As plans went ahead for Operation 'Overlord', the invasion of northern France, Ron 2 was created to serve the special needs of intelligence gathering in the run-up to the invasion. The Office of Strategic Services (OSS) needed a force of PT boats to drop off agents on the coast of enemy-occupied France, and

Below: *PT-504*, an 80ft Elco boat attached to the 34th Squadron (MTB Ron 34) which operated in support of the D-Day landings. In this photograph it appears that the boat is transporting senior officers and civilians, hence the appearance of the crew in their best blues. The boat was transferred to the Soviet Navy in December 1944. (US Navy)

Above: *PT-199* was a 78ft Higgins Boat attached to
MTB Ron 30, which served in the English Channel.
She participated in the D-Day landings, and is
photographed here transporting Admiral Harold R.
Stark to the 'Utah' beachhead. (National Archives)

to pick up sand samples from beaches, collect agents after their mission was completed
and to establish secure communication links with the French Resistance. Given the task,
the squadron would need an exceptional commander. He was found when Lt-Cdr John
D. Bulkeley, the hero of the Philippines, was appointed its first commander. The squadron
was formed in Long Island, then shipped across the Atlantic two weeks later. By 24 April
1944 the three boats were established in their new base at Dartmouth, on the south
coast of Devon.

Their first OSS mission came three weeks later, when *PT-71* was called upon to drop
agents on the Normandy coast near Cherbourg. The operation went smoothly, and the
agents were rowed ashore in a rubber dinghy without any hitch. The three boats would
conduct several similar covert missions of this kind between 20 May and 6 June, and
would continue to land agents during along the enemy-occupied portions of the French
Belgian and Dutch coasts until November.

The routine changed in early June 1944, when Ron 2 participated in the invasion of
Normandy. Reinforcements had reached Britain on the eve of the invasion, and Ron 34
(*PT-498–PT-509*, all 80ft Elco boats) played its part in the D-Day operation under the
command of Lt Allen H. Harris. Two more squadrons entered active service during the
weeks which followed; Ron 30 consisting of six 78ft Higgins boats
(*PT-450–PT-455*) commanded by Lt Robert L. Searles, and the 12 80ft Elco boats of
Ron 35 (*PT-510–PT-521*) under the command of Lt Richard Davis Jr. Another six
Higgins boats (*PT-456–PT-461*) would later reinforce Ron 30. Bulkeley was named as
the flotilla commander of the force, which now constituted 33 (later 39) boats.

The three boats of Ron 2 were attached to the command ships of the invasion fleet, where they could ferry senior officers to the beachheads. Bulkeley in *PT-71* ferried Generals Marshall, Eisenhower and Bradley ashore, during the days that followed, as well as Admirals King and Stark. Meanwhile Ron 34 was given the task of escorting the minesweepers which cleared the path to 'Utah' Beach, then placed themselves to the north, as a screen to stop any E-boat attack being made against the beachhead. The attack never came, as the Germans were taken by surprise. During the day Allied airpower ensured the E-boats stayed in port, but the risk of a night-time attack was considered a serious one. When not screening the fleet the boats were occupied rescuing survivors from mined ships, downed pilots or swamped landing craft. Only one boat, *PT-505*, was damaged during Operation 'Overlord' when she struck a mine, but she remained afloat and was able to reach port.

After 'Overlord', Bulkeley was given command of a destroyer, and Lt Harris of Ron 34 was named as the new flotilla commander. Lt Reid moved up to command Ron 34. His first chance to shine came during late August, when the boats of Ron 34 probed the ports of Brittany in search of hidden German vessels. In the process *PT-502* and *PT-504* liberated the coastal town of Morlaix on 21 August, and the crews were duly wined and feted as heroes!

The next operation was the blockade of Le Havre, a port which served as a major E-boat base. Using destroyer escorts as radar pickets, PT boats from Ron 35 and British MGBs were sent in to intercept the Germans whenever they tried to sortie from the port. Although several boats were damaged in the skirmishes which followed, no boats were lost. The Germans decided to abandon the port on 23 August, and so the Germans made a determined attempt to break out, during which *PT-511*, *PT-514* and *PT-520* managed to collectively torpedo and wreck a German torpedo-boat destroyer (destroyer escort). The German sortie was repulsed, although it would be repeated three more times before the port was captured by Allied troops, and the E-boats were scuttled.

After most of Brittany was secured the Allies decided to isolate the principal German garrisons at Lorient and St. Nazaire, as attacks on the well-fortified ports were considered too costly. Like those islands in the Pacific, the ports were left to 'wither on the vine'. The same was true of the Channel Islands, but this meant that the Germans retained naval bases on both sides of the Brittany coast until the end of the war. Clashes were inevitable, and on the night of 8–9 August *PT-509* fired a torpedo at a contact in the dark, then closed to engage the enemy with gunfire. The enemy vessel was a large German minesweeper, whose fire crippled the PT boat. Lt Harry Crist deliberately steered his boat into the side of the German ship. The minesweeper was badly crippled, but survived long enough to limp back into Jersey; all but one of the crew of *PT-509* were lost during the fight. Although there were several more skirmishes, a shortage of fuel eventually forced the Germans to stay in port, and the bases were no longer considered of any strategic importance to the Allies. The war moved on, as did the PT boats, although larger warships maintained a distant blockade of the Channel Islands and the Brittany ports until the end of the war.

After the Allied victory in Normandy and the subsequent drive through France, there was little for the PT boats to do. With no more OSS missions, Ron 2 was shipped back across the Atlantic to New York, while the surviving boats of Ron 34 and Ron 35 were transferred in batches to the Soviet Navy as part of the Lend-Lease programme, a process which began in late December 1944 and continued until the following April. The exception was the mine-damaged *PT-505*, which ended its active service at Melville, Rhode Island. The last to leave the theatre was Ron 30, which remained on active service in the English Channel until the end of the war in Europe, when the squadron was shipped back to the United States. The intention was that the squadron would be sent to

PT BASES
MEDITERRANEAN

Bône, Algeria
Advanced base; base for British Coastal Forces
Opened: 27/4/43

Bizerte, Tunisia
Base 12 — the main PT base in Med
Opened: 30/5/43

Palermo, Sicily
Advanced base, shore-based operating point
Opened: 23/7/43

Capri, Italy
Advanced base, shore-based operating point
Opened: 15/9/43

Maddalena, Sardinia
Advanced base, shore-based operating point
Opened: 1/10/43

Bastia, Corsica
Advanced base, shore-based operating point
Opened: 15/10/43

Calvi, Corsica
Advanced base, shore-based operating point
Opened: 5/44

St. Maxime, France
Advanced base
Opened: 32/8/44

Gulf Juan, France
Advanced base, shore-based operating point
Opened: 28/9/44

Livorno (Leghorn), Italy
Advanced base, shore-based operating point
Opened: 10/10/44

the Pacific, but fortunately for the crews the war ended while the squadron was being shipped home.

Although PT-boat operations in the English Channel lacked the glamour of operations in the Pacific or the Mediterranean, the three conventional squadrons who served there played a major part in the naval side of the invasion of Europe, and in the battle to wrest control of the Channel ports from the Germans. As for Ron 2, Bulkeley's three boats operated not as PT boats but as players in the clandestine world of spies, agents and intelligence gathering. Without their efforts in sampling sand from the invasion beaches, or landing agents to report on the position of coastal defences, the casualties inflicted on the troops as they went ashore on D-Day might have been significantly higher.

Below: The 80ft Elco boat *PT-140*, probably photographed off Rhode Island during crew training in late 1942 or early 1943. Later in her career she was fitted with additional deck guns and other equipment. (US Naval Institute)

PT BOAT SQUADRONS

PT boats were organised into squadrons of approximately 12 boats, although strengths varied throughout the war due to losses, availability and operational necessity. Each MTB squadron (usually abbreviated to 'Ron') usually consisted of boats of the same type, although this was not always the case. Where squadrons were not homogenous, the variants have been fully listed. Note that some boats transferred between various squadrons as the war progressed, so appear in more than one unit. However, for the most part squadrons contained boats which were all commissioned at the same time, crewed, equipped and then commissioned together as a squadron. In these cases the boat numbers within the squadron tend to be consecutive.

RON 1
Commissioned: 24 July 1940
Decommissioned 9 February 1945
Boats: *3, 4, 5, 6, 7, 8, 9* (all experimental boats), *20–31, 33, 35, 37, 39, 41–43* (77ft Elcos)
Service: Experimental Squadron, Midway, Aleutians

RON 2
Commissioned: 8 November 1940
Decommissioned: 11 November 1943
Boats: *10–19* (70ft Elcos transferred to RN during summer of 1941), *20–26, 28, 30, 32, 34, 36–40, 42–48, 59–61* (77ft Elcos), *109–114* (80ft Elcos)
Service: Panama, Guadalcanal, New Guinea
Recommissioned: 23 March 1944
Decommissioned again: 21 September 1945
Boats: *PTs 71, 72, 199* (78ft Higgins)
Service: English Channel (seconded to OSS until October 1944)

RON 3
Commissioned: 12 August 1941
Squadron lost in action during spring 1942
Boats: *PTs 31–35, 41* (77ft Elcos)
Service: Philippines
Recommissioned: 27 July 1942
Decommissioned: 7 August 1944
Boats: *21, 23, 25–26, 36, 39–40, 45–48, 59–61* (77ft Elcos)
Service: Guadalcanal, Solomons

RON 4
Commissioned: 13 January 1942
Decommissioned: 15 April 1946
Boats: *59–68* (77ft Elcos), *71–72, 199–200, 295–296, 450–452* (78ft Higgins), *95–102, 564* (78ft Huckins), *139–141, 314–317, 486–487, 505, 545, 557–559, 613, 616, 619–620* (80ft Elcos)
Service: Training Squadron, Melville RI (saw no action)

RON 5
Commissioned: 16 June 1942
Decommissioned: 15 February 1945
Boats: *62–65* (77ft Elcos), *103–114, 314–319* (80ft Elcos)
Service: Panama, Solomons, New Guinea

RON 6
Commissioned: 4 August 1942
Decommissioned: 29 May 1944
Boats: *115–126, 187–189* (80ft Elcos)
Service: Solomons, New Guinea

RON 7
Commissioned: 4 September 1943
Decommissioned: 15 February 1945
Boats: *127–138* (80ft Elcos)
Service: New Guinea

RON 8
Commissioned: 10 October 1942
Decommissioned: 28 October 1945
Boats: *66–68* (77ft Elcos), *110–114, 120–122, 129–130, 142–150, 188* (80ft Elcos)
Service: Guadalcanal, Solomons, New Guinea, Philippines

RON 9
Commissioned: 10 November 1942
Decommissioned: 24 November 1945
Boats: *126, 151–162, 187, 318–319* (80ft Elcos)
Service: Solomons, New Guinea

RON 10
Commissioned: 9 December 1942
Decommissioned: 11 November 1945
Boats: *108, 116, 124–125, 163–174* (80ft Elcos)
Service: Solomons, New Guinea

RON 11
Commissioned: 20 January 1943
Decommissioned: 11 November 1945

Boats: *175–186* (80ft Elcos)
Service: Solomons, New Guinea

RON 12
Commissioned: 18 February 1943
Decommissioned: 26 October 1945
Boats: *127, 145–146, 150–152, 187–196* (80ft Elcos)
Service: New Guinea, Philippines

RON 13
Commissioned: 18 September 1942
Decommissioned: 23 November 1945
Boats: *73–84* (78ft Higgins)
Service: Aleutians, New Guinea

RON 14
Commissioned: 17 February 1943
Decommissioned: 16 September 1944
Boats: *98–102* (78ft Huckins)
Service: Panama (saw no action)

RON 15
Commissioned: 20 January 1943
Decommissioned: 17 October 1944
Boats: *201–218* (78ft Higgins)
Service: Mediterranean

RON 16
Commissioned: 26 February 1943
Decommissioned: 26 November 1945
Boats: *71–72, 213–224, 235, 241–242, 295–301* (78ft Higgins)
Service: Aleutians, New Guinea

RON 17
Commissioned: 29 March 1943
Decommissioned: 19 November 1945
Boats: *225–234* (78ft Higgins)
Service: Hawaii, Marshalls, New Guinea

RON 18
Commissioned: 27 March 1943
Decommissioned: 1 November 1945

Boats: *103–105, 147–148, 362–367* (80ft Elcos) *368–371* (70ft Scott-Paines)
Service: New Guinea

RON 19
Commissioned: 22 April 1943
Decommissioned: 15 May 1944
Boats: *235–244* (78ft Higgins)
Service: Solomons. In mid-1944 boats were reallocated to Rons 20 and 23

RON 20
Commissioned: 3 June 1943
Decommissioned: 24 November 1945
Boats: *235–254* (78ft Higgins)
Service: Solomons, New Guinea, Philippines

RON 21
Commissioned: 8 April 1943
Decommissioned: 10 November 1945
Boats: *128, 131, 132, 320–331* (80ft Elcos)
Service: New Guinea, Philippines

RON 22
Commissioned: 10 November 1943
Decommissioned: 15 November 1945
Boats: *302–313* (78ft Higgins)
Service: Mediterranean

RON 23
Commissioned: 28 June 1943
Decommissioned: 26 November 1945
Boats: *241–44, 277–288* (78ft Higgins)
Service: Solomons, New Guinea

RON 24
Commissioned: 10 May 1943
Decommissioned: 6 November 1945
Boats: *106, 332–343* (80ft Elcos)
Service: New Guinea

RON 25
Commissioned: 17 June 1943

Decommissioned: 9 November 1945
Boats: *115, 134, 344–355* (80ft Elcos)
Service: New Guinea

RON 26
Commissioned: 3 March 1943
Decommissioned: 3 December 1945
Boats: *255–264* (78ft Huckins)
Service: Hawaii (saw no action)

RON 27
Commissioned: 23 July 1943
Decommissioned: 19 October 1945
Boats: *356–361, 372–377* (80ft Elcos)
Service: Solomons, New Guinea

RON 28
Commissioned: 30 August 1943
Decommissioned: 21 October 1945
Boats: *546–551, 378–383* (80ft Elcos)
Service: Solomons, New Guinea

RON 29
Commissioned: 22 October 1943
Decommissioned: 23 November 1944
Boats: *552–563* (80ft Elcos)
Service: Mediterranean

RON 30
Commissioned: 15 February 1944
Decommissioned: 15 November 1945
Boats: *450–461* (78ft Higgins)
Service: English Channel

RON 31
Commissioned: 5 April 1944
Decommissioned: 17 December 1945
Boats: *453–455, 462–473* (78ft Higgins)
Service: Solomons, Marianas, Okinawa

RON 32
Commissioned: 10 June 1944
Decommissioned: 18 December 1945

Boats: *474–485* (78ft Higgins)
Service: Solomons, New Hebrides, Okinawa

RON 33
Commissioned: 2 December 1943
Decommissioned: 24 October 1945
Boats: *137, 138, 488–497* (80ft Elcos)
Service: New Guinea, Philippines

RON 34
Commissioned: 31 December 1943
Decommissioned: 9 March 1945
Boats: *498–509* (80ft Elcos)
Service: English Channel. Most boats transferred to Soviet Navy in late 1944.

RON 35
Commissioned: 15 February 1944
Decommissioned: 10 April 1945
Boats: *510–521* (80ft Elcos)
Service: English Channel. Most boats transferred to Soviet Navy in late 1944.

RON 36
Commissioned: 3 April 1944
Decommissioned: 29 October 1945
Boats: *522–532* (80ft Elcos)
Service: New Guinea, Philippines

RON 37
Commissioned: 5 June 1944
Decommissioned: 7 December 1945
Boats: *533–544* (80ft Elcos)
Service: Solomons, Okinawa

RON 38
Commissioned: 20 December 1944
Decommissioned: 24 October 1945
Boats: *565–576* (80ft Elcos)
Service: New Guinea, Philippines

RON 39
Commissioned: 6 March 1945

Left: The 70ft Elco boat *PT-14* was transferred to the Royal Navy in April 1941 as part of the lend-lease agreement. She survived the war, and was returned to the USN in March 1946. This shows her British configuration, with twin 0.303in Lewis LMGs mounted in the forecastle, and a single 20mm gun aft. (Elco)

Below Left: The experimental *PT-564* was built by Higgins as a private venture and entered service in September 1943. Although she proved a well-founded design she was never adopted by the USN as a combat boat, and instead she was used as a testing vessel. (US Naval Institute)

Decommissioned 24 December 1945
Boats: 575–588 (80ft Elcos)
Service: Pacific Fleet: Philippines (no action)

RON 40
Commissioned: 26 April 1945
Decommissioned: 21 December 1945
Boats: 589–600 (80ft Elco)
Service: Pacific Fleet: Philippines (no action)

RON 41
Commissioned: 21 June 1945
Decommissioned: 6 February 1945

Boats: 600–612 (80ft Elcos)
Service: Never left home waters

RON 42
Commissioned: 17 September 1945
Decommissioned: 8 February 1946
Boats: 613–624 (80ft Elcos)
Service: Commissioned after end of hostilities, and never left home waters

RON 43
Commissioned: 12 December 1944
Decommissioned: 16 March 1945

Boats: 635–636 (78ft Higgins)
Service: Boats transferred to Soviet Navy, April 1945

MTB RON 44
Boats: 761–772 (78ft Higgins)
Service: Squadron never commissioned

MTB RON 45
Boats: 783–784 (78ft Higgins)
Service: Squadron never commissioned

Opposite Above: This 78ft Higgins boat has had her armament augmented by two extra pairs of single 20mm guns, one forward of the bridge, the other astern of the .50cal turrets. (US Navy, courtesy of PT Boaters Inc., Battleship Cove, Fall River, MA)

Opposite Below: *PT-10*, the first of the 70ft Elco boats, during sea trials off New York. This Scott-Paine design became the basis for all subsequent Elco-A boats. She entered service in November 1940, and was transferred to the RN under lend-lease in April 1941. (US Navy)

Left: 70ft Elco boats *PT-11* and *PT-18* were completed in November and December 1940 and transferred to the RN in early 1941. When transferred they were fitted with British LMGs. (Elco)

Below: Higgins boats of Ron 13 off Attu in the Aleutians on 21 June 1943. Alongside the quay is destroyer USS *Gillis* (AVD-12) and behind her a PBY Catalina. (National Archives)

EQUIPMENT, MARKINGS AND CAMOUFLAGE

Above: Most – but not all – PT boats were fitted with two or four depth charges, and could be used as makeshift anti-submarine vessels. However, it was soon found that these could be used as anti-surface weapons, by dropping them in the path of an enemy vessel and setting the depth setting to explode in shallow water. This Type C weapon carried a 300lb explosive charge. (US Navy, courtesy of PT Boaters Inc., Battleship Cove, Fall River, MA)

EQUIPMENT

After the USN's round of competitions, the production of experimental boats, and the running of sea trials, the Scott-Paine design adopted by Elco was considered the clear winner of all PT-boat types on offer. Following the adaptation of the design to fit the USN's standard type of torpedo, Elco began to produce 77ft PT boats in its New Jersey boatyard, and it was these boats which were used to create the USN's first operational squadrons. Higgins Industries of New Orleans also produced a PT boat, while the USN also commissioned a limited number of 78ft boats from Huckins of Jacksonville. However, while the Higgins design proved reliable enough, after the summer of 1942 the mainstay of the PT-boat fleet became an improved Elco design, the 80ft boat. It is worth examining the four basic types of wartime operational PT boats in a little more detail. Please note that the armament given for these boats is only a general guide, as squadron commanders and even individual boat commanders added and removed guns as they saw fit, experimenting with their weapons' fit to suit their operational needs. The weapons listed here represent the standard weapons' fit, but as a glance at the photographs will show, this was little more than a general guideline.

The Elco 77ft PT boat

When the initial 70ft Elco was evaluated by the USN, it was found to be an ideal boat, except that it was too small to shoot the standard 21in torpedoes and their attendant torpedo tubes. Therefore plans for a lengthened and improved version of the original vessel were produced, and the USN duly authorised Elco to go into mass-production with their new design. The keel of *PT-20* was laid in October 1940, and it entered service nine months later. 29 of these boats, *PT-20* to *PT-48* entered service between June and September 1941, and by the time the Japanese attacked Pearl Harbor, three squadrons of the boats were available for service, in Rons 1, 2 and 3.

During the summer of 1941 Elco laid down another 20 boats, although ten of these were earmarked for service in the Royal Navy, despite being allocated PT-boat numbers (*PT-49–PT-58*), and all would see extensive service in the Mediterranean, where they served as Britsh MTBs. The remaining 10 boats, *PT-59–PT-68* entered service early in 1942. During the Solomons campaign of 1943, *PT-59*, *PT-60* and *PT-61* were converted into gunboats by removing their torpedoes and adding four extra twin .50cal machine guns and two 40mm Bofors guns to each boat. This was a response to the operational demands of barge-busting, and gave these vessels an armament superior to that of the more modern 80ft Elcos in the same theatre.

PT boat numbers: *20–48, 59–68* (*PT-48–PT-58* were transferred to the Royal Navy).
Number to enter service: 39
Length: 77ft
Beam: 19ft 11in
Draught: 4ft 6in
Displacement: 46 tons
Propulsion: Three 1,200hp Packard engines
Maximum speed: 42kts
Complement: 2 officers, 8 men
Armament (as fitted):
PT-20–PT-43: Two twin .50cal MGs in Dewandre turrets; Four 21in Mk VIII torpedoes
    (in Mk XVIII launchers)
PT-44–PT-48, PT-59–PT-68: Dewandre turrets replaced by standard Mk XVII twin MG
    mounts. Single 20mm gun added aft

Above: The first of many, *PT-1* was built by the Fogal Boat Yard for the Miami Shipyard Corporation in 1941. Like her sister *PT-2*, this 58ft boat was purchased by the USN for evaluation, but was almost immediately reclassified as Small Boat *C6083*, as she was considered unsuitable for active service. (PT Boat Museum)

The Elco 80ft PT boat

Although these vessels were similar to the 77ft boats which had preceded them, they were based around a largely new design. Apart from being 3ft longer, these vessels were heavier, slightly slower and certainly less manoeuvrable. This was balanced by improved stability as a weapons platform, and in their improved sea-keeping abilities. Their plywood hulls were stronger than their predecessors, their crew quarters were better and they were better able to sustain damage than the 77ft boats. While their original displacement was set at 38 tons, by the time these vessels were given their full suite of weapons, this standard displacement had increased to around 51 tons, or 56 tons when fully laden.

The keel of *PT-103*, the first 80ft Elco boat was laid down less than two months after Pearl Harbor, in late January 1941, and the boat entered service in June 1942. Production continued at an average rate of 8–12 boats per month until the end of the

Above: From the start of 1945 onwards, new Elco boats were fitted with a small dory or wherry, which was mounted on the forward bridge roof. *PT-588* entered service in April 1945, and was attached to the 39th Squadron (MTB Ron 39), which served in the Pacific. (US Navy)

Opposite Above: *PT-340* and other 80ft Elco boats of MTB Ron 24–25, which operated in the southwest Pacific from the summer of 1943 onwards. (US Navy)

Opposite Below: In this modification tried out on the experimental 78ft Higgins Boat *PT-564* (known as 'Hellcat'), two twin 0.50cal machine guns have been fitted in the bow, where control cables allow them to be fired from the safety of the bridge. Similar field-modified systems were used in the Pacific. (US Navy)

war, although *PT-603–PT-624* (begun in early 1945) were not placed into service before the end of the war. At that point orders for *PT-731–PT-790* were cancelled while they were still under construction, and the majority of them were shipped out to the Soviet Union in kit form during December 1945 to fulfil a Lend-Lease agreement.

Elco continued to modify its original design as the war progressed, and a range of different weapons' fits were devised for these boats. From 1943 onwards basic surface-search radar sets were fitted to most new boats, and due to the experiences gained during the first year of the war in the Pacific, modifications were made to the armament. The most significant improvement was the replacement of torpedo tubes with launching racks, and Mk VII or Mk VIII torpedoes with the lighter, more reliable, Mk XIII models. The lightweight launching racks were introduced following experiments at Melville, Rhode Island, held during 1943, and the new device was considered a great improvement. The torpedo was simply rolled over the side rather than fired, at which point its own motor would drive it towards the target. By the time the boats fitted with torpedo racks rather than torpedo tubes began entering service in late 1943 (*PT-486* on), many of the boats already in service had already been modified, and their tubes replaced by racks. Not only did this save weight and create space, but it also reflected the diminishing role of the torpedo in PT-boat warfare.

While early 80ft boats had either two or four 21in torpedoes in tubes, their replacement with torpedo racks led to a weight saving, which in turn allowed the addition of more conventional firepower to the boats. While early boats were fitted with two single 20mm guns and two twin .50cal machine guns, many later boats replaced at least one of their 20mm guns with a 40mm piece. Most boats were modified in the field, where the most popular change was the mounting of a 37mm gun (originally supplied to the USAAF) in place of one of the other 20mm or even 40mm pieces, as its high rate of fire was considered to be a boon. Later in the war most boats were fitted with multiple rocket launchers and sometimes an infantry light mortar was added for close-in attacks against targets on the shore. Even Japanese 23mm anti-tank guns found their way onto the forecastles of some PT boats in the Pacific, showing the extent some captains took their search for extra or improved weapons for their boats. From *PT-115* on, all boats carried smoke generators, and all Elco boats (77ft and 80ft) were capable of being fitted with 2–4 depth charges.

PT boat numbers: *103–196, 314–367, 372–383, 486–563, 565–600 (PT-601–PT-624* and *PT-731–PT-790* were ordered, but not delivered before the war ended)
Number to enter service: 296
Length: 80ft
Beam: 20ft 8in
Draught: 5ft 3in (By 1945, changes to the weapons fitted to the boat meant that the displacement was officially 61 tons, the draught 5ft 6in, and the speed reduced to 41kts)
Displacement: 50 tons
Propulsion: Three 1,200hp Packard engines, later increased first to 1,350hp then 1,500hp Packard engines.
Maximum speed: 43kts
Complement: 2 officers, 9 men (later increasing to 3 officers and 14 men)
Armament (as fitted):
PT-103–PT-383: Two twin .50cal MGs in Mk XVII turrets; Four 21in Mk VIII torpedoes (in Mk XVIII launchers); Single 20mm gun (aft)
PT-486–PT-555: Two twin .50cal MGs in Mk XVII turrets; Four 22.5in Mk XIII torpedoes (in Mk I racks); Two single 20mm guns (one forward, one aft)

PT-556–PT-600: Two twin .50cal MGs in Mk XVII turrets; Two 22.5in Mk XIII torpedoes (in Mk I racks); Two single 20mm guns (one forward, one aft)

Note: There were the exceptions to the rule, such as *PT-174* which had a 40mm gun fitted on her forecastle, or some that omitted one or other of their 20mm guns. *PT-556* was fitted with a 20mm 'Thunderbolt' mount, and other vessels were retro-fitted with the same weapon after it proved useful in combat.

The Higgins 78ft PT boat

Although these vessels lacked the graceful lines of the Elco boats (one critic describing them as boxes with a point on the end), they proved versatile PT boats, and were popular with their crews. *PT-71* entered service in late July 1942, and the Higgins Yard produced an average of 6–10 boats per month until the end of the war.

Although their specifications were similar to the Elco 80ft design, the Higgins boats were slightly different in several aspects such as their turning circle which was tighter, and their speed, which was slightly slower. Although not such good sea

boats as the Elcos, these Higgins boats had less cluttered upper deck spaces, which meant it was easier to adapt them to other purposes, such as landing troops, agents or stores. The crew quarters were more cramped than in the Elcos, but the engines were more accessible. Unlike the first Elcos, the Higgins boats used all three engines simultaneously to drive three propeller shafts, rather than keeping one in reserve for idling, as was the case with the Elcos. Although these differences gave these boats a slightly different performance than their counterparts, they operated in exactly the same way, and shared the same range of missions.

Originally the boats were designed to carry the Mk VII or Mk VIII torpedo and its attendant torpedo tube, but from *PT-197* on, the boats entered service with Mk XIII torpedoes and Mk I torpedo racks, which made these vessels even more spacious. While deck armament changed as much as it did on Elco boats, the later boats were better armed than the early Higgins vessels.

PT boat numbers: *PT-71–PT-94, PT-197–PT-254, PT-265–PT-313, PT-450–PT-485*. In addition *PT-564* was an experimental variant produced as a private venture by Higgins. It was retained for evaluation by the USN, but was never used as an operational boat. *PT-625–PT-660* were ordered, but not delivered before the war ended.
Number to enter service: 146
Length: 78ft 6in

Above: A 40mm Bofors gun mounted in the stern of a 70ft Elco boat. The Swedish-designed gun was the most widely used AA gun of the war, but on PT boats it provided a heavy punch against surface targets. It had an effective range of approximately 7,500 yards, and a rate of fire of more than 60 rounds per minute. (US Navy)

Above Right: The bridge of *PT-522*, an 80ft Elco boat which entered service in March 1944. By raising the height of the twin .50cal turrets and spacing them down the hull of the boat on alternate sides, the gunners were given a greatly improved field of fire compared to earlier port and starboard mounts (US Navy)

Right: From 1943 onwards, PT boats were fitted with radar and other pieces of electronic equipment, which gave the vessels a useful edge in combat. *PT-588*, a very late-war 80ft Elco boat, carried a radar mounted inside the dome on her foremast, a second exposed radar mounted above it, a radio direction-finding antenna, an IFF (identification of friend or foe) antenna, plus a full suite of radio masts mount. (US Navy, courtesy of PT Boaters Inc., Battleship Cove, Fall River, MA)

Left: The Elco 'Thunderbolt' was a design which incorporated mountings for two belt-fed .50cal machine guns and four drum-fed 20mm guns in one single mounting. The prototype was fitted to *PT-136*, and later versions omitted the machine guns, and modified the mounting. Although the Thunderbolt' provided a heavy volume of fire, the system proved unpopular due to the awkward nature of the mount. (Electric Boat Company)

Below: There was a tendency for crews to add additional armament to their vessels whenever they could. This unidentified 80ft Elco boat stationed in the Pacific during 1945 carries her 21in Mk XIII torpedoes, a twin .50cal and a single 20mm gun in the bow, another twin .50cal machine gun in a turret to the right of the bridge and a pair of Mk 50 rocket launchers on each side of her forward hatch. Another twin .50cal is mounted on her starboard beam, and a 20mm gun is mounted on her port side. She probably carried a 37mm or 40mm gun aft, as well as depth charges. Finally a small 60mm mortar is placed on top of her bridge. (National Archives)

Beam: 20ft 1in
Draught: 5ft 3in
Displacement: 43 tons
Propulsion: Three 1,350hp Packard engines (1,500hp engines were fitted from 1944 on)
Maximum speed: 40kts
Complement: 2 officers, 9 men (later increasing to 3 officers and 14 men)
Armament:
PT-71–PT-94: Two twin .50cal MGs in Mk XVII turrets; Four 21in Mk VIII torpedoes (in
    Mk XVIII launchers; Single 20mm gun (aft)
PT-197–PT-313: Two twin .50cal MGs in Mk XVII turrets; Four 22.5in Mk XIII torpedoes
    (in Mk I racks); Two single 20mm guns (one forward, one aft)
PT-450–PT-485: Two twin .50cal MGs in Mk XVII turrets; Two 22.5in Mk XIII torpedoes
    (in Mk I racks); Two single 20mm guns (one forward, one aft); One 40mm gun (aft)

The Huckins 78ft PT boat

Another 78ft boat, the Huckins Yacht Works vessel was considerably lighter than the Elco
or Higgins boats, and was never considered suitable for operational use. The vessel is
mentioned here largely because these craft served as training vessels at the PT boat
School at Melville, Rhode Island, and two other groups of Huckins boats served:
PT-98–PT-104 served in the Panama Canal Defense Zone, while *PT-255–PT-265* were
stationed at Pearl Harbor. In either case the vessels could have been deployed for
operational use if required, so it is worth mentioning them alongside the combat vessels
of the PT boat fleet. The Jacksonville firm had established its reputation before the war
producing 'rum runners', and the design of these vessels reflected the profile of these
civilian vessels. Their superstructure was minimal, giving the boats a distinctive 'box-like'

Below: The loading of a Mk. VII torpedo on board a
77ft Elco boat. *PT-64* is seen in the background; part
of MTB Ron 5 which served in the southwest Pacific.
This photograph was taken at Melville, RI, when
PT-64 formed part of the training squadron,
MTB Ron 4.
(US Navy)

silhouette, but even more noticeable was their hull, which was designed to plane in the same way as many British MTBs, as opposed to the Elco and Higgins designs which tended to cut their way through the water like a conventional vessel.

PT boat numbers: *PT-95–PT-102, PT-255–PT-264*
Number to enter service: 18
Length: 78ft
Beam: 19ft 5in
Draught: 5ft
Displacement: 42 tons
Propulsion: Three 1,350hp Packard engines
Maximum speed: 43kts
Complement: 2 officers, 9 men
Armament (when fitted): Two twin .50cal MGs in Mk XVII turrets; Four 21in Mk VIII torpedoes (in Mk XVIII launchers); Single 20mm gun (aft)

MARKINGS & CAMOUFLAGE

In theory, every operational PT boat carried its boat identification number where it was clearly visible. During the prewar years, the number was often painted on the forward portion of the vessel's hull, prefixed by 'PT'. These were at least 30in high, and the white lettering was embossed in black, to create a somewhat three-dimensional impression.

Above: There was a large degree of variety between the weapons' fit of boats in active service, as commanders added new weapons, or moved their existing weaponry around. In the nearest boat the 37mm gun has been moved further aft on the forecastle, replacing the 20mm gun. Which was moved forward into the bow position. The remaining boats of the squadron have their guns mounted in the more conventional position with the 37mm in the bow, and the 20mm behind it. (US Navy)

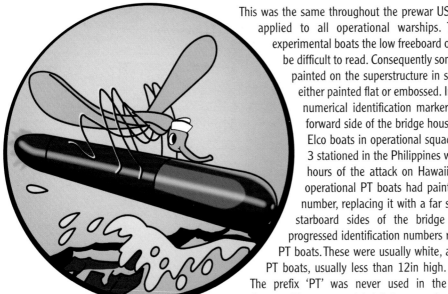

Above: The 'Mosquito Fleet' — this roundel was the basis for many squadron badges.

Right: *PT-196*, the last of the 80ft Elco series, entered service in May 1943, and served in the southwest Pacific. She entered service sporting this unusual camouflage scheme, consisting of a series of light and dark grey stripes, with a shark's face design on her bow, together with the name *Elcopuss*. The boat reverted to a more conventional camouflage scheme when she reached her operational squadron, MTB Ron 12. (US Navy)

Below Right: *PT-170*, an 80ft Elco boat, entered service in December 1942, serving in the South Pacific. In this photograph she is camouflaged using the Adaptor Pattern (also known as the Zebra Pattern) of black and white stripes, with light blue-grey shading. On active service the white stripes were replaced by yellow-green ones, but by mid-1943 at the latest the boat had reverted to conventional grey. (Elco)

This was the same throughout the prewar USN, where a similar lettering system was applied to all operational warships. There were exceptions, as on some experimental boats the low freeboard of the vessel meant that this system could be difficult to read. Consequently some boats had their identification numbers painted on the superstructure in smaller white or sometimes black letters, either painted flat or embossed. In addition, most boats also had a smaller numerical identification marker without the 'PT' prefix painted on the forward side of the bridge housing. This system held true for all the 77ft Elco boats in operational squadrons before Pearl Harbor, including Ron 3 stationed in the Philippines which would be thrust into the war within hours of the attack on Hawaii. Within days of 7 December 1941, all operational PT boats had painted out their highly visible identification number, replacing it with a far smaller identifying mark on the port and starboard sides of the bridge superstructure. However, as the war progressed identification numbers reappeared on the forward hulls of many PT boats. These were usually white, and far smaller than those of the prewar PT boats, usually less than 12in high.

The prefix 'PT' was never used in the wartime marking system. A brief glance at the photographs in this book will show that there was little standardisation regarding the painting of identification numbers in the PT-boat fleet, and the final decision was often left with individuals such as flotilla commanders, base commanders or even individual boat captains.

Another common feature on most PT boats was the addition of a roundel bearing the squadron emblem. While not always carried, these were common in the prewar 'mosquito fleet', and became increasingly popular as the war progressed, and the number of squadrons multiplied. These roundels varied in size, but were most commonly 12in or so in diameter, and were mounted on either side of the bridge superstructure, or further aft if there was no suitable space. The design of the roundels usually took the form of a cartoon, featuring a torpedo, a PT boat image, or commonly the squadron number. This said, several squadrons — Rons 1, 2, 6, 7, 10 and 26 — all shared the same apt design; the image of a mosquito flying over the waves carrying a torpedo. As this book is concerned primarily with the operational performance of the 'mosquito fleet' rather than its appearance, there is insufficient space to cover markings and emblems in any great detail. For those seeking more information on the subject, the website of the PT Boat Museum is a mine of information on such matters.

Above: Ron 34 squadron roundel.

Above Right: Loading ammunition at a forward PT boat base in the South Pacific, 1943–44. *PT-174,* the 80ft Elco boat in the foreground was probably the only PT boat to carry a 40mm gun mounted on her forecastle. (US Navy)

Right: The 80ft Elco boat *PT-588* entered service too late to see any action, but if she did, she carried the right tools for the job. This represents the final configuration of the standard armament of a wartime Elco boat; a single 37mm gun in the bow, with a single 20mm gun and a Mk 50 rocket launcher mounted towards the rear of the forecastle. A 40mm Bofors was mounted in the stern, and two twin .50cal turret-mounted machine guns were fitted abaft the bridge. She also carries lightweight mounts for four Mk XIII torpedoes. (US Naval Institute)

When they first entered service, most PT boats were painted in Standard Navy Gray (note US spelling). Below this was a thin black waterline mark, while the lower hull was red, the colour of the Copperoyd bottom enamel used as an anti-fouling agent on all PT boats and other small warships in the USN. Draught marks were white below the waterline, and black above it. Decks were also painted grey. Other schemes for brand new boats included overall Dark Gray, or Navy Gray (a mid blue-grey colour). Apart from boats sporting an overall grey scheme, decks were usually painted Deck Gray which was darker than Standard Navy Gray, or else they were given the even darker Dark Gray colour. This meant that even when they were first sent into operational service, boats often sported slightly different colour schemes. By 1942, the majority of Elco boats appear to have entered service painted with a Tropical Green base.

However, the nature of PT boat warfare meant that it was considered important that the boats remain undetected by the enemy before they were ready to launch an attack. Boats berthed in forward PT-boat bases were often camouflaged if the threat of an enemy air attack was considered to be high. Camouflage nets were used when available, otherwise the moored or berthed boats were covered with fronds and branches cut from the shore. In the Pacific theatre this method of temporary camouflage inevitably led to the introduction of unwanted visitors on board; cockroaches, lizards and rats.

Naturally the same emphasis — to avoid detection — meant that camouflage was applied to the hulls of the boats themselves. The camouflage of PT boats was undertaken for one purpose: making the boats harder for enemy lookouts or pilots to spot them. If this bought the boat and her crew a few vital seconds in combat, then the camouflage scheme was well worth the effort. Numerous camouflage schemes were used by PT boats during the war, most of which were developed by the Bureau of Ships, a USN department headed by Capt Henry A. Ingram. However, fleet commanders, flotilla commanders and squadron commanders were all given some degree of leeway to adapt the approved camouflage schemes to suit local operating conditions, or even to reflect the availability of paint. It is therefore, difficult to provide a completely accurate description of the schemes used by operational PT boats, although we can provide a general outline.

The Bureau of Ships provided over 12 different camouflage schemes for Elco boats which were worked out jointly by the department and by Elco's own camouflage team. While Higgins Industries offered suggestions to the Bureau of Ships, they appear to have left the design of camouflage for their boats up to the experts. Where possible the bureau would provide drawings of the schemes, and then it was up to the crews to follow them or to adapt them somewhat. For example, in mid-1943 the Bureau reacted to requests from operational PT-boat commanders to come up with a green-based scheme suitable for use in the waters of the Solomons chain. The result was Measure 31, which used a combination of Navy Green and Ocean Green on the hull, and a base of Deck Green on the horizontal surfaces. The hull was painted with a base of the lightest Ocean Green then overlaid with swirling patches of the darker green and black. The same two dark colours were also applied to the deck. When the crews were ready to apply the camouflage, it was decided to vary the scheme slightly, so that no two boats in the same squadron had exactly the same pattern. The crews liked this scheme, because the base green provided a robust cover which helped hide the normal wear and tear to the paintwork these boats experienced, at least when compared to the light grey base colour provided by Standard Navy Gray. Eventually 12 PT-boat squadrons in the South Pacific theatre were painted using Measure 31.

While it was unusual for camouflage schemes to be applied to the horizontal deck areas, which were usually painted Deck Gray or Deck Green during 1942, by mid-1943

PT Boats in US Naval Service

1–2	58ft Fogal (experimental) Crouch design
3–4	58ft Fisher (experimental) Crouch design
5–6	81ft Higgins (experimental) Sparkman & Stephens design
7–8	81ft Philadelphia Navy Yard (experimental) Bureau of Ships design
9	70ft Scott-Paine (experimental)
10–19	70ft Elco (experimental) Scott-Paine design
20–48	77ft Elco
48–58	77ft Elco. Transferred to Royal Navy on completion
59–68	77ft Elco
69	72ft Huckins. Reclassified as *YP-106* (Patrol Yacht), September 1941
70	76ft Higgins. Reclassified as *YP-107*, September 1941
71–84	78ft Higgins
85–87	78ft Higgins. Transferred to Soviet Navy, February 1943
88	78ft Higgins. Transferred to Royal Navy, April 1943
89	78ft Higgins. Transferred to Soviet Navy, February 1943
90–94	78ft Higgins. Transferred to Royal Navy, April 1943
95–102	78ft Huckins
103–196	80ft Elco
197	78ft Higgins. Transferred to Soviet Navy, February 1943
198	78ft Higgins. Transferred to Royal Navy, April 1943
199–54	78ft Higgins
255–264	78ft Huckins
265–276	78ft Higgins. Transferred to Soviet Navy, November 1943
277–288	78ft Higgins
289–294	78ft Higgins. Transferred to Soviet Navy, December 1943
295–313	78ft Higgins
314–367	80ft Elco
368–371	70ft Canadian Power Boat Company (Scott-Paine design). Built for the Dutch Navy, but transferred to USN in May 1943
372–383	80ft Elco
384–399	70ft Vosper. Transferred to Royal Navy on completion, May 1944
400–449	70ft Vosper. Transferred to Soviet Navy on completion, February 1944
450–485	78ft Higgins
486–563	80ft Elco
564	78ft Higgins ('Hellcat' – experimental vessel)
565–600	80ft Elco
601–622	80ft Elco. War ended before vessel entered active service
623–624	80ft Elco. Construction cancelled due to end of hostilities
625–660	78ft Higgins. War ended before vessels entered active service. *PT-625–PT-656* transferred to Soviet Navy, May 1945
661–692	70ft Vosper. Transferred to Soviet Navy on completion, May 1945
693–730	Transfer to Soviet Navy cancelled due to political reasons, August 1946
731–760	80ft Elco. Transferred to Soviet Navy in pre-fabricated kit form before completion, October 1944
761–790	80ft Elco. Construction cancelled due to end of hostilities
791–796	78ft Higgins. Transfer to Soviet Navy on completion cancelled due to political reasons, October 1946
797–808	78ft Higgins. Construction cancelled due to end of hostilities

both the Bureau and crews were becoming more adventurous in extending the camouflage scheme to cover all visible surfaces of the boat.

Another popular scheme was the Adaptor System devised by Lt-Cdr George C. Evans. With this scheme the boat was covered by a series of parallel 'zebra' stripes, in black and white, or black and light blue grey (Haze Gray). Boats using this pattern painted their decks a dull blue. The scheme was designed to confuse the enemy trying to judge ranges, and at ranges of over a mile it amazingly made the boats much harder to see. The Adaptor System was particularly associated with Higgins boats, and Ron 15 used this scheme in the Mediterranean. Crews in the Pacific soon adapted it to permit the boats to blend in against a jungle shore by replacing the black and white stripes with black and light green (Haze Green). In these cases the decks of the boats were painted Deck Green.

In some cases boats were simply painted a different colour than Standard Navy Gray as a means of adapting to their combat environment. For instance Measure 1 was simply a dark grey version of the normal non-camouflaged Standard Navy Grey scheme, where the whole boat was painted in the darker colour. Measure 3 was similar but lighter than the standard scheme (known as Light Gray), although the deck was painted in Standard Deck Gray, a slightly darker shade than the Standard Navy Gray. Measure 8 involved starkly angled patches of Light Gray and the darker bluey-grey Ocean Gray colour, while the deck and parts of the superstructure were painted Deck Blue. Other popular schemes — such as Measure 13, which was a combination of blues and greys — were often applied on top of existing paintwork, although the crews often ignored or did not have access to official patterns. This created what could best be described as 'field-applied' camouflage schemes, bearing only a passing resemblance to the schemes devised by the Bureau of Ships. Most boats had several different paint schemes applied during their operational life, and changes were rarely recorded. Therefore the best method of determining the schemes used by certain boats or squadrons at specific times is by examining the photographic evidence, comparing the tones in the black and white images with those of vessels whose colour scheme is better recorded, such as on larger surface warships. Like so much in the private world of the PT boats, rules were often ignored, as effectiveness in action outweighed smartness and uniformity whilst in port.

Insert left: The aft port-side 21in torpedo rack of a 77ft Elco boat. Before the boat went into action the dome covering the muzzle of the torpedo launcher was unlatched and stowed below decks. (US Navy)

Below: Loading a 21in Mk VII torpedo into the starboard bow tube of *PT-65*, a 77ft Elco boat which entered service two months after the attack on Pearl Harbor. This photograph was taken in the Motor Torpedo Boat Training Center at Melville, RI in October 1942. (United States Naval Historical Center)

THE CREW

While much could be said of individual PT-boat commanders, the nature of life in the 'mosquito fleet' emphasised the role of teamwork. Unlike the commander of a submarine, the often very junior officers who commanded PT boats frequently worked in tandem with other boats, where operational control of the group was given to the senior officer present. Within the boats themselves discipline was far less noticeable than on larger ships in the fleet, and an almost democratic attitude tended to prevail. This said, the CO of the boat was the man whose decisions could spell success or disaster for his boat and crew, so by necessity he remained somewhat aloof from his men. These men needed to be resourceful, intuitive and willing to use their initiative. They were often left to their own devices, taking responsibilities which were unheard of for junior officers on larger ships.

The first PT-boat officers — like John Bulkeley — were almost all line officers in the USN rather than naval reservists. This meant that they were graduates of the US Naval Academy at Annapolis, Maryland, and had been officers in the prewar USN during the late 1930s.

After Pearl Harbor this all changed. From

Above: A group of officers on board *PT-66*, a second series 77ft Elco boat which entered service in January 1942, and which served in the southwest Pacific. This photograph was taken in 1945, by which time she was relegated to the transport of senior officers and other VIPs. Deck stiffeners which were a feature of the later 77ft boats can be seen running along the outside of the cabin, on the main deck. (US Navy)

then on, the majority of PT-boat officers came from the US Naval Reserve. Reservist officer training centred around Midshipman's School, a form of naval reserve training course undertaken while at college. After 90 days, these officer candidates were given reserve commissions. The majority of PT boat commanders and executive officers (XOs) were Naval Reserve officers.

By 1944 only 5% of wartime naval officers in the 'mosquito fleet' were regular academy-trained graduates, and most of these officers served as senior commanders, or as flotilla base or task group staff. PT-boat officers were therefore almost exclusively reservists, former civilians (usually students) who had a sufficient grounding in pleasure boating or sailing to qualify as entrants in the Midshipman's School programme. It was then up to the USN to turn these officers and the men they would command into professional PT-boaters.

When the US Navy established its PT-boat arm during early 1941, it faced the problem that there was no MTB training facility for PT-boat officers and men. A stop-gap solution was the appointment of the tender USS *Niagara* as a training ship, and the former yacht was duly berthed at the Naval Torpedo Station at Newport, Rhode Island, where it became both a support boat for PT boats and a training centre for their young regular navy commanders. Lt William C. Specht was placed in charge of training, and he developed the blueprint for the courses which would follow. When the USS *Niagara* was sent to Pearl Harbor in August 1941, Specht and his students were not only left without a base, but most of them, including their training officer were sent to the Pacific when Ron 1 was ordered to join the Pacific Fleet. However, by that stage enough PT boats had entered service for the USN to designate one of them a non-operational formation, dedicated to training future PT-boat commanders. This meant that MTB Squadron 4 (Ron 4) commanded by Lt-Cdr Alan R. Montgomery became the training squadron, based at Newport. The boats and their attendant base offices served as the nucleus for the training programme until 17 February 1942, when the USN decreed that an MTB Squadrons Training Center would be established at Melville, Rhode Island. Newly promoted to lieutenant-commander, Specht was shipped back from Hawaii to take command of the training facility. He achieved miracles at Melville, and by late March 1942 the Training Center was ready for business. MTB Ron 4 was officially attached to Melville as its training squadron, and the process of training naval officers and enlisted men to run PT boats began in earnest in early April.

As for the sailors themselves, until December 1942, all enlisted men in the USN were volunteers, as conscription was only introduced in January 1943. These volunteers had to be single, aged 17 to 25, high school graduates – and white (or Hispanic). Until 1942 African-Americans were only enlisted as mess stewards and cooks, and it was not until late 1943 that coloured crewmen began to appear in the 'mosquito fleet'. During the war the upper age limit for enlistment was increased to 35. Similarly, while the prewar basic training course for sailors lasted for 16 weeks, this was reduced to just four weeks in January 1942. Having been trained to 'salute, drill and jump to orders', sailors were detailed to further schooling in their speciality before being sent on to serve in the fleet. Usually these sailors had to have

Above: The Scott-Paine designed 70ft long *PT-369* was originally built in Canada for the Dutch Navy, but was turned over to the USN in May 1943, following the surrender of the Dutch East Indies. The gunner in the foreground is manning a bow-mounted 37mm auto-cannon. (National Archives)

some practical naval experience on larger ships before they were allowed to specialise in PT boats, although this requirement was waived during 1943 due to the increased demands of the service.

The training course for officers and enlisted men lasted for eight weeks, but in the summer of 1943 it was lengthened to three months, to provide additional training based on combat experience. A repair training unit was also created at Melville, where crews learned to repair their own boats. For the most part instructors were veteran PT-boat men, who were able to share their combat experiences with the trainees, while a string of guest lecturers regaled the students with their own view of the PT-boaters' private war. The size of the Training Center also continued to expand throughout the war. Melville became a sizeable town of huts, with accommodation for students and staff, plus offices and support facilities for Ron 4, a fuel depot, small dry docks, a torpedo shop, plus all the usual attributes of a training establishment such as mess halls, drill halls, athletic fields and eventually even a swimming pool (as it was discovered most trainees couldn't swim). By late 1943 Melville could process 90 officer trainees and 860 enlisted men per course, so it was able to produce trained crews at almost the same rate as Elco and

Above: *PT-596*, an 80ft Elco boat which entered service in May 1945, and was sold seven months later. Her Mk 50 rocket launchers have been swung down into the firing position while her crew man the boat's more conventional weapons, a 37mm, a 20mm and two twin 0.5in machine guns. (US Navy)

Opposite Bottom: The crew of the 80ft Elco boat *PT-331* stands by to engage Japanese shore positions with the 40mm gun mounted on the quarterdeck of their boat. This engagement took place in support of a small amphibious landing on the island of Tong, in the Admiralty Islands in March 1944. (National Archives)

Higgins were producing boats for them to serve in. By the time the war ended, just under 1,800 officers and 12,000 enlisted men had passed through its training programme, and had gone on to fight in operational squadrons in all theatres of war.

As well as being a training facility, Melville also dealt with the administration of the PT-boat army of the USN, assigning crews to boats, and dealing with all the personnel needs of the 'mosquito fleet'. The staff at Melville usually assigned replacement crewmen to flotilla or base commanders, for allocation as required, although it was mid-1943 before the system really began to work effectively. Usually the surviving crew of damaged or destroyed boats remained in the theatre, and were allocated by their squadron or flotilla commanders as they deemed necessary to keep their remaining boats fully crewed.

Although PT boats varied in size and design, a similar crew was carried on all boats although this standard complement was increased as the war progressed. The 80ft Elco were built with crew berths for three officers and 14 men, one officer and five men more than the official complement. However, by late 1943 the size of the crew was increased, and by 1944 every berth was filled. By comparison a 78ft Higgins boat also had space for three officers and 14 men, while the smaller, lighter Huckins boats could only carry a maximum of two officers and 10 enlisted men. While some jobs such as engineering were specialised, most crewmen were generally cross-trained in several jobs, especially gunnery. However, compared with the crew on larger warships, the PT-boaters were badly served, having to make one of their number into the boat's cook, regardless of his culinary abilities. With limited storage space and virtually no refrigerators, fresh food was at a premium. Spam in various forms was often the staple diet. As the novelist James A. Michener recalled of life in PT boats:

'It was just damned dirty work, thumping, hammering, kidney-wrecking work. Even for strong guys from Montana it was rugged living. No bakery was aboard. In fact bread was often as scarce as beef-steak.'

Above: The crew quarters in PT boats were incredibly cramped, and both officers and enlisted men shared the same mess space for meals. (Smithsonian)

Scrounging became the standard way of augmenting the monotonous diet, and if it were not for the relative freedom from naval regimen, PT boats might have envied their fellow sailors in the battleships and cruisers. While conditions might have been spartan, the majority of PT-boat crews wouldn't have swapped their assignments for all the comfort of a larger ship if the offer was made.

PT Boat Losses

Boat	Cause	Place	Date
PT-33	Grounding	Pt. Santiago	15/12/41
PT-31	Grounding	Subic Bay	20/1/42
PT-32	Scuttled	Sula Sea	13/3/42
PT-34	Airplane	Cauit Island	9/4/42
PT-35	Demolished	Cebu Island	12/4/42
PT-41	Scuttled	Mindanao	15/4/42
PT-44	Surface Craft	Pacific	12/12/42
PT-43	Surface Craft	Guadalcanal	10/1/43
PT-112	Surface Craft	Guadalcanal	10/1/43
PT-28	Grounding	Alaska	12/1/43
PT-37	Surface Craft	Guadalcanal	1/2/43
PT-111	Surface Craft	Guadalcanal	1/2/43
PT-123	Airplane	Guadalcanal	1/2/43
PT-67	Explosion	New Guinea	17/3/43
PT-119	Explosion	New Guinea	17/3/43
PT-165	Submarine	New Caledonia	23/5/43
PT-173	Submarine	New Caledonia	23/5/43
PT-22	Weather	Pacific	11/6/43
PT-153	Grounding	Solomons	4/7/43
PT-158	Grounding	Solomons	5/7/43
PT-166	Airplane	Solomons	20/7/43
PT-117	Airplane	Rendova	1/8/43
PT-164	Airplane	Rendova	1/8/43
PT-109	Surface Craft	Blackett Straits	2/8/43
PT-113	Grounding	New Guinea	8/8/43
PT-219	Weather	Attu	9/43
PT-118	Grounding	Vella Lavella	7/9/43
PT-172	Grounding	Vella Lavella	7/9/43
PT-136	Grounding	New Guinea	17/9/43
PT-68	Grounding	New Guinea	1/10/43
PT-147	Grounding	New Guinea	19/11/43
PT-322	Grounding	New Guinea	23/11/43
PT-239	Fire	Solomons	14/12/43
PT-145	Grounding	New Guinea	4/1/44

Boat	Cause	Place	Date
PT-110	Collision	New Guinea	26/1/44
PT-279	Collision	Bougainville	11/2/44
PT-200	Collision	Rhode Island	22/2/44
PT-251	Gunfire	Bougainville	26/2/44
PT-337	Gunfire	New Guinea	7/3/44
PT-283	Gunfire	Bougainville	17/3/44
PT-121	Airplane	New Britain	27/3/44
PT-353	Airplane	New Britain	27/3/44
PT-135	Grounding	New Britain	12/4/44
PT-346	Airplane	New Britain	29/4/44
PT-347	Airplane	New Britain	29/4/44
PT-247	Gunfire	Bougainville	5/5/44
PT-339	Grounding	New Guinea	27/5/44
PT-63	Explosion	New Ireland	18/6/44
PT-107	Explosion	New Ireland	18/6/44
PT-193	Grounding	New Guinea	25/6/44
PT-133	Gunfire	New Guinea	15/7/44
PT-509	Surface Craft	English Channel	9/8/44
PT-202	Mine	France	16/8/44
PT-218	Mine	France	16/8/44
PT-555	Mine	Mediterranean	23/8/44
PT-371	Grounding	Molukkaa Passage	19/9/44
PT-368	Grounding	Halmahera N.E.I.	11/10/44
PT-493	Surface Craft	Surigao Strait PI	25/10/44
PT-320	Airplane	Leyte	5/11/44
PT-301	Explosion	New Guinea	7/11/44
PT-321	Grounding	San Isadoro Bay	11/11/44
PT-311	Mine	Corsica	18/11/44
PT-363	Gunfire	Halmahera	25/11/44
PT-323	Airplane	Leyte	10/12/44
PT-300	Airplane	Mindoro Island	18/12/44
PT-73	Grounding	Philippines	15/1/45
PT-338	Grounding	Mindoro Island	28/1/45
PT-77	Surface Craft	Luzon	1/2/45
PT-79	Surface Craft	Luzon	1/2/45

Below: A 21in Mk VII/VIII torpedo weighed 2,600lb, and was an ungainly 21ft 4in long. The weapon entered service before World War I, and by 1942 it was considered outclassed by more modern weapons. It had a range of approximately 3,500yd at 35kts. (US Naval Historical Center)

Below Right: In contrast to the Mk VII, the 21in Mk XIII torpedo weighed 2,000lb, but was just 14ft 4in long, a third less than its predecessor, although it carried a similar explosive charge and an improved propulsion system. Based on the weapon developed for naval torpedo bombers, it had a range of 6,300yd at 35kts. (US Naval Historical Center)

Top Right: PT-333 on trials off New York, 20 August 1945. (National Archives)

Above Right: PT-463 seen making a high-speed run without torpedoes in 1944. (National Archives)

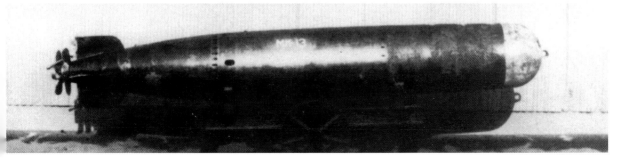

POSTWAR

When the war ended in mid-August 1945, the USN had 30 MTB squadrons in commission, consisting of approximately 384 PT boats. Of these, six were in the Pacific fleet, while 19 were serving in the 7th Fleet, which was now serving under Admiral Nimitz rather than General MacArthur. This was because the entire American command in the Pacific was gearing itself up for an invasion of the Japanese mainland, codenamed Operation 'Olympic'. Due to the dropping of the atom bomb on Hiroshima and Nagasaki, the invasion never took place. The PT-boat crews were spared this last, potentially brutal final campaign. At the time, four more squadrons were in the United States, readying themselves for their part in Operation 'Olympic', but were destined never to leave home waters. These included two squadrons which had been shipped over from Europe following the defeat of Germany. Finally there was Ron 4, the training squadron based in Melville, Rhode Island. In addition, others still on the stocks were in various states of completion in the Elco and Higgins yards when hostilities finally ended.

When the last shots were fired, the 'mosquito fleet' found itself out of a job. The USN considered these craft to be expendable in action, and a similar attitude prevailed once the fighting ended. The boats had done their job, but because of their all-wood construction, the USN was reluctant to mothball them for use in some future conflict, which it did for most of the rest of its surface fleet. The majority of the boats still being built had their construction contracts cancelled, although those nearing completion at the end of the war were finished and delivered. There is no evidence that any of these vessels were ever fitted out as combat-ready boats.

During September and October 1945 the USN surveyed the remaining boats in service, the majority of which were deployed in the Philippines. Almost half the boats were deemed to be too battered to retain in service. Some of the older boats had simply outlived their useful service life, as their engines and hulls were in poor condition after nearly four years of constant service. While the anti-corrosion paint applied to the underside of PT-boat hulls went some way to protecting them from the attentions of harmful marine creatures, many boats were found to be damaged below the waterline by the attentions of the teredo worm, while in some boats their upper works suffered from dry rot or termite damage. These boats had been kept in operation due to the necessities of combat, and with the prospect of an invasion of Japan it was assumed that every available boat would be needed. Peace meant that these largely unserviceable boats were considered unfit for active duty.

Of all the boats the USN surveyed in the Philippines, almost half were considered too battered to remain in service. A total of 118 PT boats was eventually condemned for a variety of reasons, including combat damage, or structural faults such as cracked frames keels or spacers. In mid-October the order came to strip these vessels of anything valuable such as guns, equipment, engine parts and valuable fittings, then the vessels were gathered on the Philippine island of Samar for disposal. By this time the total had increased by three vessels to 121 PT boats of various types. Starting on 1 November the beached hulls of these valiant little boats were systematically burned in a series of bonfires which continued for six weeks as boats were destroyed in batches. While no sailor likes to see the wanton destruction of his vessel, for the PT-boaters this Wagnerian end to their craft also meant an end to the war. It represented their own survival as a crew, and the chance to return home to waiting families. It also symbolised victory.

Most of the surviving boats which passed inspection were also disposed of by the USN, but their fate would be significantly less spectacular. The PT boats had proved their worth in combat, and at least some of them represented a marketable asset. During the months which followed some of the newer vessels would be sold or transferred overseas, either singly or in batches, the recipients including the Philippine Navy, the Argentinian Navy and the Cuban Navy. The Soviet Navy had already been the recipient of a substantial number of boats, but the Lend-Lease programme to Russia ended when the relationships between the two countries soured in late 1945, and all further shipments were cancelled. In May 1946 many of the remaining boats were stripped of their weaponry and were then sold out of service by the US Maritime Commission. These craft were bought by private firms or individuals, and the boats they purchased were destined to end their days as fishing vessels, charter boats, pleasure craft, dive boats, salvage vessels and even as ferry boats. While most of these are no longer afloat after six decades, a few still remain as a tangible reminder of their dramatic early life.

With just a handful of exceptions the USN removed the weapons and fittings from its remaining boats, then reclassified them from PT boats to 'small boats' in the summer of 1946, becoming little more than multi-purpose tenders and launches for use in the USN's main bases. By 1948 the majority of these were stripped of their engines, and were reclassified as 'floating equipment', which was the USN's way of categorising

Below: They were expendable. After the war, the bulk of the PT boats which had served so well during the Pacific campaign were rounded up on the island of Samar, and in November 1945 they were stripped of valuables, then destroyed. By that stage many hulls were in poor condition, and it was felt they had no further service life left in them. (National Archives)

Above: Many medals were awarded to the men of the 'mosquito fleet'. There were Presidential Unit Citations for Rons 12 and 21; an Army Distinguished Unit Citation for Ron 3; Medals of Honor for Lt John D. Bulkeley and Lt-Cdr A. Murray Preston; and Navy Crosses (as illustrated above) for 22 officers and men, including Bulkeley.

Right: The 0.50in (.50cal) Browning machine gun was a magazine-fed weapon, and employed a curved feed system, although the exact style of feed and mount varied. The majority were turret-mounted, where the ammunition feed came from curved boxes sited inside the turret. In this photograph the twin .50cal weapon is elevated to its full angle of 80°. (US Navy, courtesy of PT Boaters Inc., Battleship Cove, Fall River, MA)

obsolete vessels that were not worth the expense of mothballing, yet which still retained some value for accounting purposes, like stacks of office supplies and stationery. Over the following years a handful would be transferred to the smaller NATO forces such as the Royal Norwegian Navy, while others were sold or scrapped.

The USN decided to retain just two operational squadrons of 80ft Elco boats, Rons 41 and 42, both of which were units still in the United States when hostilities ended. Finally, the training squadron at Melville — Ron 4 — was kept in service and Rons 41 and 42 were attached to it, the three formations becoming TF.23.4. However in April 1946 the USN decided to decommission these squadrons, retaining just four PT boats in active service; *PT-613*, *PT-616*, *PT-619* and *PT-620*, all of which were 80ft Elco boats. These were redesignated as part of the Navy's Operational Test and Development Force, and remained in service until the Korean War, when they were transferred to the South Korean USN.

Today, just a handful of these PT boats remain in existence. The PT Boaters Inc. and the PT Boat Museum have identified 18 former PT boats which have survived in various states of repair around the world. Many boats in commercial hands have been greatly modified over the years, having their hulls shortened, their superstructure and internal spaces changed and their engines replaced with more economical diesels rather than gasoline-driven fuel-hungry Packards. Of the largely unmodified vessels, the 80ft Elco boat *PT-617* and the 78ft Higgins boat *PT-796* are both on display at the PT Boat Museum at Battleship Cove, Fall River, Massachusetts. Neither saw service during the war. *PT-617* was sold to a private owner then purchased by the PT Boaters Inc. in 1979, while *PT-796* being transferred from Higgins to the USN, then being stored as 'floating equipment' until it was rescued by PT Boaters Inc. in 1970. Both vessels have now been fully restored.

Another Higgins boat, *PT-658*, was designated as 'floating equipment' for a decade before being sold. In 1993 the boat was purchased by Save the PT Boats Inc., then fully restored. She is now on display at the Naval Reserve Center on Swan Island, near Portland, Oregon.

PT-728 was a British-designed Vosper MTB, built in Annapolis Maryland as part of the Lend-Lease programme, and completed just after the end of the war. It was originally intended to send her to the Soviet Union, but the Lend-Lease programme was cancelled before she could be shipped overseas. As the Royal Navy had no use for her, the USN sold her in mid-1947. Today she survives as a privately owned vessel, owned by the Conch Republic Rum Company of Key West, Florida. The boat has been restored to resemble her original intended appearance, and now serves as the official flagship of the highly unofficial 'Conch Republic Navy', and serves as such during the annual 'Conch Republic Celebrations' on the island. In effect she has become a promotional party boat. However, PT-728 was responsible for sparking the author's interest in PT boats, when he first saw her a decade ago, while working as the curator in a Key West museum.

Finally there is the *PT-309*, a 78ft Higgins boat which is the only surviving restored PT boat to have seen active service. Completed in late January 1944, she served as part of Ron 22 in the Mediterranean theatre, seeing action in the Tyrrhenian and Ligurian Seas during 1944-45. In June 1948 she was sold out of service, but in 1995 the vessel was purchased by the Admiral Nimitz Museum and Historical Center, in Fredericksburg, TX. The vessel has now been fully restored, and plans are afoot to display her next to the battleship USS *Texas* in the Battleship State Historic Park in La Porte, Texas. This small handful of restored boats, plus a few virtually unrecognisable other survivors, are now all that remains of the 'mosquito fleet'. At least the majority of these vessels are now safely in the hands of organisations dedicated to preserving both the vessels themselves, and the memory of the men who served in the PT boat fleet.

ASSESSMENT

Just how effective were the PT boats of the 'mosquito fleet' during World War II? Did they measure up to what was expected of them, and did the craft exert a significant influence on the course of the naval war against Japan, Germany and Italy?

In purely analytical terms the boats were not particularly effective in doing the job they had been designed for, but this was balanced by the discovery of new roles where the boats could prove exceptionally useful. Almost every attempt to use PT boats as vehicles to launch torpedoes at enemy shipping proved singularly unsuccessful, and in the large majority of attacks the torpedoes failed to damage the enemy ships targeted. In most cases the 'fish' missed their target completely, or else the torpedo turned out to be faulty.

While the USN tended to blame this failure on the inadequate training of its PT-boat crews, the body of evidence against the torpedo itself was mounting. By mid-1943 evidence from PT-boaters, submariners and destroyer crews all attested to the reliability of Japanese torpedoes, and the faulty nature of the American version of the weapon. It was hard enough for torpedo boats to hit their target anyway, as they had to fire along the bearing of their boat. This meant 'leading' the enemy vessel slightly, approaching it at an acute angle, then firing the torpedo so it would converge with the spot the enemy ship would be in when the two paths converged. While on paper the effective range of the torpedo

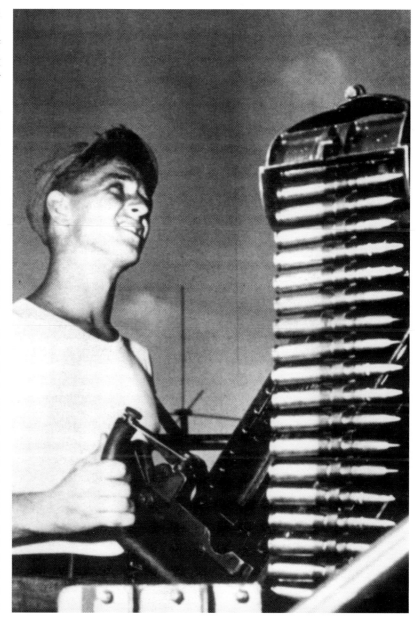

Above: The bridge of *PT-522*, an 80-foot Elco boat which entered service in March 1944. By raising the height of the twin .50cal turrets and spacing them down the hull of the boat on alternate sides, the gunners were given a greatly improved field of fire compared to earlier port and starboard mounts (U.S. Navy)

was 10,000yd, with a top speed of just 27kts (slower than a speeding destroyer), the boat had to fire its torpedo spread at a far shorter range if it was to reduce the margin of error enough to hit the target. This meant that a PT boat speeding towards (or rather slightly ahead of) an enemy at 40kts would have to close within 2–3,000yd or even less, and the timing of the attack had to be judged to perfection. The USN sent its PT boats to war with the Mk VIII or Mk XIV torpedo, both of which dated from World War I. A firing charge was used to launch the torpedo from its tube (a compressed air system was used on Higgins boats), the charge detonated when the commander engaged an electrical contact on the bridge. If this failed a crewman would hit the firing mechanism with a mallet.

The trouble was, even if a perfect firing solution could be obtained, the chances of actually hitting the target remained slim. After the dismal performance of American torpedoes in the first years of the war, a series of tests revealed that in two out of three firings, the torpedo proved to be faulty, and missed the target. The most common failure was in the depth setting, and it was discovered that 'fish' set to run at a set depth would consistently run deep, often 10–12ft below the prescribed depth. This mean that if a PT boat fired its torpedoes at a surface target such as an enemy destroyer, transport or barge, even if the depth was set at shallow, the 'fish' would pass underneath the target without hitting it. However, this was only part of the problem. American torpedoes were set with a proximity device which allowed it to explode when it was close to a target. The idea was that even if the torpedo would ordinarily miss, it could still explode close enough to do some damage to the target. Unfortunately it was discovered that these devices were even more temperamental than the depth settings, and torpedoes could explode as much as a thousand yards short of their target, or simply not explode at all. Another less common failure was to the steering mechanism, and instead of running straight and level, the torpedo would steer an erratic course, which in some cases even meant looping around in a circle back towards the firing boat. The proximity problem was dealt with by deactivating the mechanism, turning the torpedo into a device designed to explode on contact. This still left the depth setting and occasionally erratic steering mechanism, and it was not until 1944 that both problems were effectively dealt with. This meant that for much of the war, the main weapon of the PT boats was too unreliable to guarantee its effectiveness in combat.

As the war progressed, it was discovered that while PT boats had been designed as torpedo delivery systems, their most effective role came when the patrol part of their name was emphasised. They proved to be highly effective high-speed interceptors, capable of engaging enemy transport barges and small craft at night, and the boats were capable of ranging deep into enemy-held waters to undertake these interdiction missions. Their speed meant that by daylight when enemy air activity became a problem, the boats could be back in friendly waters, or in a forward PT-boat base, ready to launch another patrol the following evening. With the introduction of radar to the boats, and improvements in the quality of the sets, the boats had a significant edge over the Japanese, who were forced to rely on their night-vision to evade enemy patrols. The boats could be vectored onto a target, then use their array of deck guns to destroy the enemy vessels. This was the tactic perfected by American PT-boat commanders off New Guinea, then honed in the Solomons and the Philippines. Against better-armed targets, it also proved its worth in the waters of the Mediterranean. While this role was not what the boats had been designed for, it was what they were good at.

PT boats were designed as a type of fast attack vessel, with a limited operational role. While commanders still had to decide whether the boats should work as an independent unit or as part of a coordinated fleet, their use was a tactical one. They were considered expendable naval assets, and by sinking enemy warships they could tip the balance in a naval battle. The trouble was, the days of climactic naval battles were past.

Instead, the PT boat became something even more useful. It became a strategic tool, like the heavy bomber, the aircraft carrier and the submarine. Its role in interdicting enemy coastal supply routes, in helping deny enemy strongholds the food and ammunition they needed to resist was a strategic mission, and one which fitted perfectly into the strategy devised for winning the war in the Pacific. This allowed the PT boat to 'punch well above its weight', and to play a significant part in America's victory. As torpedo boats, these craft were mediocre, but as gunboats, they were without equal, capable of taking the fight to the enemy in waters too shallow for larger warships.

From Leghorn to Luzon they fought their own private war against enemy coastal traffic, and in so doing they earned their place in history as one of the most effective strategic naval weapons of the war.

Below: Four 77ft Elco boats of MTB Squadron 3 en route to the Philippines on board the USN oiler *Guadalupe*. This method of transport was commonplace, as the boats were considered too small to make large transits under their own steam. (US Navy)

REFERENCE

The PT Boat Page

I searched the Web for information about PT Boats and came up pretty dry so I decided to start a page dedicated to the men who served in the "Mosquito Fleet" during World War II. It struck me that many people out there may not even have seen the sitcom McHale's Navy, let alone heard anything about what PT Boats were and what part they played in the war.

The PT Boat was a small, wooden craft that carried enough firepower to sink a battleship, was faster than anything on the water, and could sneak right up to shore to perform reconnaissance or drop off troops. For a more detailed list of specifications, check out my PT Specs page.

My father served in the English Channel during World War II on PT 507, an 80' Elco Boat. He was part of Squadron 34. Here is 'Ron 34's logo that decorated their boats.

WW II PT Boats, Bases, Tenders

- About Us
- Join Us
- News
- PT Boat Vets
- E-Cards
- Message Board
- Ship's Store
- Museum
- Reunion Information
- NEW Wallpapers
- PT Boat Information; Knights of the Sea
- PT Boat Plans & Photos
- PT/Other Links

FIFTY TONS OF FIGHTING FURY

PT BOATS · BASES · TENDERS

DETAILED PT BOAT INFORMATION SECTION

World War II PT Boats Museum and Archives
This web Site Copyrighted © 2003 & 2004 by PT Boats, Inc.

This site was last updated 05/18/2004

MEMBER

Lieutenant John F. Kennedy, USN

Related Information
- Transcript of Naval Service
- Citation for Navy and Marine Corps Medal
- Report on Loss of PT-109, copy of original document
- Information on PT-109 and Patrol Torpedo Boats
- History of PT-109
- Photographs of PT-109
- Bibliography

"Any man who may be asked in this century what he did to make his life worthwhile, I think can respond with a good deal of pride and satisfaction, 'I served in the United States Navy,'" wrote President John F. Kennedy in August 1963. A former naval officer, Kennedy was born in Brookline, Massachusetts on 29 May 1917 to Rose and Joseph P. Kennedy. After attending public schools in Brookline, Kennedy went on to The Choate School in Wallingford, Connecticut, and attended the London School of Economics from 1935 to 1936. Kennedy graduated cum laude from Harvard University in 1940 and began graduate school with the help of Captain Alan Kirk, the Despite having a bad back, Kennedy was able to join the U.S. Navy through the U.S. Naval Attache in London when Joseph Kennedy was the Ambassador. In October 1941, Kennedy was appointed an Ensign in the U.S. Naval Reserve and joined the staff of the Office of Naval Intelligence (ONI) who had been the Naval Attache in London when Reserve and joined and briefing information for the Secretary of the Navy and other top officials. On 15 January 1942, he was assigned to an ONI field office in Charleston. The office, for which Kennedy worked, prepared intelligence bulletins and at Chelsea, Massachusetts. After completing his training, South Carolina. After spending most of April and May at Naval Hospitals at Charleston Illinois, from 27 July through 27 September. After completing this training, Kennedy entered the Motor Torpedo Boat Squadron his training 2 December, he was ordered to the training squadron, Motor Torpedo Squadron FOUR, for duty as the Commanding Officer of a motor torpedo boat, PT 101, a 78- foot Higgins boat. In January 1943, PT 101 with four other boats was ordered to Motor Torpedo Boat Squadron FOURTEEN, which was assigned to Panama.

WEBSITES

www.battleshipcove.com
The PT Boat Museum, Battleship Cove: see below under Museums.

www.ptboats.org/
PT Boats Inc., PO Box 38070, Germantown, TN 38183
Tel: (901) 755-8440 Fax: (901) 751-0522

Founded by former PT-boat crewmen, PT Boats Inc. is a charitable organisation run by veterans as a way of preserving the history and legacy of PT boats, and the men who served in them. Based just outside Memphis, Tennessee, PT Boats Inc. maintains an archive of personal memoirs, technical specifications and other pertinent documentation which helps tell their story. They also maintain a small library and archive which may be viewed by appointment, and they maintain a small mail order business. The site of PT Boaters Inc., this website contains a host of great information, including boat specifications, a squadron history, a shop, and most importantly, an on-line collection of hitherto unpublished personal accounts and published references to PT boats in action. Finally the organisation publishes a biannual magazine.

www.tpwd.state.tx.us/park/battlesh/facilities.htm
Battleship Texas State Historical Park: see below under Museums.

www.indiodesign.com/pt658/index.htm
The US Naval Museum, Washington Navy Yard, Washington DC: see below under Museums.

www.history.navy.mil/
US Naval Historical Center: see below under Museums.

www.nationalgeographic.com/pt109/
There are many sites relating to JFK and PT-109. The National Geographic site is good, as is the US Naval Historical Center's (www.history.navy.mil/faqs/faq60-2.htm)

FURTHER READING

Buckley, Robert J.: *At Close Quarters*; US Navy, Naval History Division, Washington, 1962.

Campbell, John: *Naval Weapons of World War II*; Conway Maritime Press, London, 1985.

Chun, Victor: *American PT Boats in World War II*; Schiffer Publishing, Atglen, PA, 1997.

Donovan, Robert J.: *PT-109: John F. Kennedy in WW II*, McGraw-Hill, New York, 2001 (first published 1961).

Connely, T. Garth: *PT Boats in Action*; Squadron/Signal Publications (Warship Series, No. 7), Carrolton, TX, 1994.

Ferrel, Robert; *US Mosquito Fleet*; PT Boat Museum, Newport, RI, 1977.

Ferrel, Robert & Ross, Al: *Early Elco PT Boats*; PT Boat Museum, Newport, RI, 1980.

Friedman, Norman: *US Naval Weapons*; Naval Institute Press, Annapolis, MD, 1982.

Friedman, Robert: *US Small Combatants*; Naval Institute Press, Annapolis, MD, 1982.

Hoagland, Edgar D.: *The Sea Hawks: With the PT Boats at War: A Memoir*; Presidio Press, Novato, CA, 1999.

Keresey: *PT 105*; Naval Institute Press, Annapolis, MD, 1995.

Lambert, John & Ross, Al: *Allied Coastal Forces of World War II. Vol. II: Vosper MTBs and US Elcos*; Conway Maritime Press, London, 1993.

Manchester, William: *American Caesar*; Little, Brown & Co, Boston, MA, 1959.

Morison, Samuel Eliot; *History of United States Naval Operations in World War II vols II–IX, XIII*; Castle Books, Edison, NJ, 2001 (first published 1947–54).

Polmar, Norman & Morison, Samuel L.: *PT Boats at War: World War II to Vietnam*; MBI Publishing, Osceola, WI, 1999.

Tredinnick, Frank & Bennett, H.: *An Administrative History of PTs in World War II*; unpublished archive manuscript, US Naval Historical Center, Washington DC, 1945.

MUSEUMS

The PT Boat Museum, Battleship Cove

Battleship Cove, 5 Water Street, Fall River, MA 02722-0111
Tel: (508) 678-1100 Fax: (508) 674-5597

Battleship Cove is a major historical attraction whose collection centres around the battleship USS *Massachusetts*. However, in addition to a range of other historical vessels and a museum dedicated to destroyers, the site is also home to the PT Boat museum.

The museum is run by PT Boats Inc., whose collection includes the 80ft Elco boat *PT-617* and the 78ft Higgins boat *PT-796*. The PT Boat Museum also includes displays and artefacts covering the operational history of the PT-boat squadrons, and examples of weapons, equipment and personal memorabilia. Battleship Cove has a PT Boat Coordinator (Donald Shannon), and the centre provides a range of related special exhibits and special events such as veterans days and lectures. Battleship Cove also maintains a well-stocked gift store, which contains an extensive range of PT-boat related merchandise. However, it is suggested you call ahead for up-to-date information on opening times and special events before your visit.

The National Museum of the Pacific War

Admiral Nimitz State Historic Site, PO Box 777, Fredericksburg, TX 78624
Tel: (830) 997-4379

Website: http://www.nimitz-museum.com/index.htm

Located in Fredericksburg, Texas the museum is located near the boyhood home of Admiral Nimitz, and is part of the Admiral Nimitz State Historic Site. The parent museum includes several offshoots including the Admiral Nimitz Museum, an extensive aviation museum and the Center for Pacific War Studies. Although the museum owns the only surviving wartime PT boat, the 78ft Higgins boat *PT-309*, the vessel is currently being restored, and it is planned to display her at another site in La Porte, Texas. This museum contains displays and archives covering the PT-boat war in the Pacific, and static displays are supported by a range of special exhibitions and other events.

Battleship Texas State Historical Park

3427 Battleground Road, La Porte, TX 77571
Tel: (713) 479-2411

The home of the Second World War battleship USS *Texas*, the State Park outside Houston, Texas is also planning to be the new home of *PT-309*, which is apparently being restored on the site. Details of her expected completion date is still unavailable. The Park is also the site of the Battle of San Jacinto (1836).

The US Naval Museum, Washington Navy Yard, Washington DC
Save the PT Boat Inc.

A group of PT-boat veterans and their supporters in Oregon formed a charitable organisation in order to restore PT-658, a 78ft Higgins boat. The group plans to make her the centrepiece of a new naval museum. Currently the boat is stored at the US Navy and Marine Corps Readiness Center at Swan Island, OR, and is only available for viewing by prior arrangement.

US Naval Historical Center

805 Kidder Breese SE, Washington Navy Yard, Washington DC 20374-5060
All relevant phone numbers are listed on the Center's website.

Based in the historic Washington Navy Yard, the Center incorporates a superb museum dedicated to the history of the US Navy, and an extensive archival facility. In addition the Navy Yard is a historic attraction in its own right, and includes numerous open air displays of ordnance and other large objects, as well as being the home of the US Marine Corps Museum. However, heightened security means that access in now restricted to bona-fide researchers and visitors, and passes have to be arranged prior to any visit. Both the museum and the archives contain items relevant to the PT boat story.

Left: During the summer of 1943 the USN developed a simple torpedo release system where the Mk XIII weapon could be released directly over the side of the boat, rather like a depth charge. The device was fitted to 80ft Elco boats operating in the southwest Pacific, and later became standard in many late-production PT boats (National Archives)

INDEX